LIKEWISEWORSHIP.COM

DO
LIKEWISE

REDISCOVERING THE PURPOSE
OF THE WORSHIP PASTOR

JUSTIN UNGER ▶ JOSH JAMES

© 2020 by Likewise Worship Inc.

1st Edition

Published by The Likewise Group

Edited by Kent DelHousaye, Co-Founder of the Love & Transformation Institute

Cover & Interior Design by Michael Koelsch / Koelsch Studios

Printed by Jostens

All Scripture quotations, unless otherwise indicated, are taken from the Holy Bible, New American Standard Bible, and English Standard Version

All emphases in Scripture quotations have been added by the authors.

ISBN: 978-0-578-41117-0

For Jesus.
Our Chief Shepherd who knows just what we need!

PRAISE FOR
DO LIKEWISE

"This book is the worship manual for all worship leaders who want to be more than just musicians and vocalists. It's a must read for anyone who wants to truly shepherd the church through music. I hope Do Likewise becomes the go-to textbook for the next generation of worship pastors."
-- *Dr. Kent DelHousaye - Co-Founder of Love and Transformation Institute. Boise, ID*

"Anyone who wants to lead people, not just in singing, but in authentic, passionate, biblically anchored worship of God needs to read this book and listen carefully to the wise counsel Justin and Josh have to offer. This can transform your church and will minister deeply to your own soul."
-- *Bob Lepine, co-host FamilyLife Today & Lead Pastor at Redeemer Church, Little Rock, AR*

"When the culture is trying to push us into performance with small thoughts of the kingdom, being saturated in the profound and deep affections of God for His bride is the only hope for worship leaders to follow the call to serve Christ and others with open hands. This worship pastors guide is a faithful work in pointing the way."
-- *Tim Maughn - Co Lead Pastor of Redemption Church. Gilbert, AZ*

"I hope everyone who worships Jesus reads this book! Worship leaders have a difficult job in every culture and time. But in today's church culture with so much spectator, consumer, entertainment, self-centered thinking, leading worship may be harder than ever. Worship leaders need tender hearts and spines of steel made that way by the transforming work of the Spirit and the Word of God. In this book, Justin and Josh have given the church a gift that is profoundly challenging, encouraging, practical and biblical. Satan hates worship and he has caused much strife and division over our churches and followers of Jesus. Reading this book will help clear away so much of the noise, confusion, and idolatry that "worship wars" have caused."
-- *Erik Thoennes, Professor and Chair of Theology, Talbot School of Theology/Biola University Pastor, Grace Evangelical Free Church, La Mirada*

"Justin and Josh do a fabulous job of delving into the heart and life of being a worship pastor. Their casual approach drew me into a deeper understanding and appreciation for their convictions about leading this experience for believers. Loved it!"
-- *Dr. Tim Griffin, Vice President, Grand Canyon University*

"True worship in a local church requires both a skillful hand and a heart filled with integrity. The hard-earned wisdom Justin and Joshua offer here can help unify the church, end the worship wars, and raise up healthy, humble worship pastors. I just wish this book existed 10 years ago!"
-- *Bruce Garner - Senior Pastor @ Crosspoint Church, Huntington Beach, CA*

CONTENTS

For God is not unjust so as to forget your work and the love which you have shown toward His name, in having ministered and in still ministering to the saints. And we desire that each one of you show the same diligence so as to realize the full assurance of hope until the end, so that you will not be sluggish, but imitators of those who through faith and patience inherit the promises. HEBREWS 6:9-12

Throughout this book, you will notice two distinct voices. Justin Unger and Josh James serve with Likewise Worship, a nonprofit ministry that aims to disciple and develop healthy and humble worship pastors who have been called by God to serve in the local church. Their voices are distinguished by font and writing style as they communicate their collective passion for worship and the unity of the Body of Christ.

Justin's writings are in bold print and Josh's writings are in thin print.

To learn more about the vision and mission of Likewise Worship, and how you can get involved visit: **www.likewiseworship.com**

At one point on this journey, Josh and I were seeking wisdom on a few challenging issues as we began to launch Likewise Worship. We decided to reach out to our dear friend and "wise church owl," Darryl DelHousaye. Darryl is the Chancellor at Phoenix Seminary and has been so influential and supportive of our worship mission over the years. When Josh and I were sitting in his office at the seminary, he shared with us a simple but profound encouragement from Psalm 13 that cut deep into our hearts and helped us put into perspective why we do what we do. We thought it would be encouraging for you to hear from his heart.

DARRYL
DELHOUSAYE

Why a Worship Leader?
[Psalm 13]

Let me ask you a question. Are there times that you feel God is a million miles away? I am asking you, as a worship leader, because many of you who are guiding in worship might sometimes feel abandoned by God. It is especially important to know what you are attempting to accomplish through leading a congregation in worship today because the great temptation is to become a worship performer rather than a worship leader. True worship expresses both praise and gratefulness for God's engagement in our lives by giving us, as individuals, yet another opportunity to feel His presence touching our souls.

Some are coming to worship God in the midst of great pain. They come with the same question C.S. Lewis asked after losing the love of his life in his book, *A Grief Observed*. He agonized: "Where is God? Go to Him when your need is desperate, when all other help is vain, and what do you find? A door slammed in your face and a sound of bolting and double bolting on the inside.

After that, silence. You may as well turn away. The longer you wait, the more emphatic the silence will become."

Have you ever asked, "Where is God?" We say we believe in God, but do we trust what we believe? The psalmist tells us in Psalm 139 that the presence of God is always with us from the outermost darkness to the innermost womb of our mother. So, if God feels a million miles away, maybe an even better question to ask is, "Who moved?"

What do we do when doubts rise up in our souls, and we have questions about His presence with us? The 13th Psalm addresses this very issue. The Psalm has three stanzas with two verses each: the problem (13:1-2); the petition (13:3-4); and the praise (13:5-6).

David most likely composed this Psalm while he was either running from Saul or later when his son Absalom conspired against him. This Psalm was even set to music by the German composer Johannes Brahms in the late 19th century. Yes, the same one who wrote Brahms' Lullaby. In this context, comfort is not found in a sweet melody but in a profound truth.

THE PROBLEM

"How long, O Lord? Will you forget me forever? How long will you hide your face from me? How long must I take counsel in my soul and have sorrow in my heart all the day? How long shall my enemy be exalted over me?" Psalm 13:1-2 (ESV)

The cynics might think we are simple minded because we believe in a God who cares for us. Are they right? Four times in these first two verses the question is asked: "How long? How long? How long? How long?" How long, God, do I have to wait?

Does God actually forget us, and hide His face from us? Pagan litany says: "There is no God, and if there is a God, He's forgotten you anyway." God counters this philosophy with profound truth: "Even to your old age I am He, and to gray hairs I will carry you. I have made, and I will bear; I will carry and will save." Isaiah 46:4 (ESV)

When David speaks of "taking counsel in my soul," it may be better translated "wrestle in my soul." How long do I have to wonder: Are you there, God? It does seem like heaven is "bolted and silent" at times.

Again, God counters with His Word: "Wait for the Lord; be strong, and let your heart take courage; wait for the Lord!" Psalm 27:14 (ESV)

What does waiting do? In distress we often think: "No one cares and maybe our critics are right. We are simple minded believing there is a God who cares." Why would David trust what he believed about God even when he was feeling God had forgotten him? In this instance, waiting is a form of perseverance that demonstrates loyalty to a relationship, and trust in that relationship. We know that David trusts God because in verses 3 and 4 he is praying. Why is he praying?

THE PETITION

"Consider and answer me, O Lord, my God: light up my eyes, lest I sleep the sleep of death, lest my enemy say, 'I have prevailed over him,' lest my foes rejoice because I am shaken." Psalm 13:3,4 (ESV)

David asks to have his "eyes enlightened" because his vision is blurred. Just like a cataract causes the lens of the eye to become progressively opaque, David is in desperate need of a clear view of God. His struggle is not with God but with the cloudy vision he has of Him. In this same manner, we often let the way that we feel cloud our view of God. Our eyes are deceived to believe in a God who is less than He is. By enlightening our eyes, our faith is strengthened because God is the author of faith. Remember, Jesus said it was the Father in heaven who causes us to recognize the truth of His Son (John 6:44-45). Peter even tells us that faith is a gift from God Himself (2 Peter 1:1).

David's prayer essentially is: "I need this restoration of new sight before my faith dies." David had a long standing history on the battlefield where wounded men did not have a medic to care for them or a stretcher to take them to safety. The picture here is of a man lying mortally wounded who will "sleep the sleep of death" unless there is an intervention.

The skeptic says, "Maybe my antagonists are right. There is no one who cares, no help, no encouragement, and no hope.

In this cold indifferent universe, I am an accident on a speck of a planet, and there is no God out there." But, anger and bitterness does not help me!

David prays: "Oh Yahweh, my God." This is a confession of faith. Unless God does something to restore his sight, he will be dead. He is basically saying, "God, show me You are there and that I have not been abandoned. My spiritual cataracts need healing. Even though I am filled with anxiety, please give me a new view of Yourself, of my God who does not abandon His own."

THE PRAISE

"But I have trusted in your steadfast love; my heart shall rejoice in your salvation. I will sing to the Lord, because He has dealt bountifully with me." Psalm 13:5,6 (ESV)

When life is strained, praise becomes a forgotten impulse. David now demonstrates trust in what he believes and will make a vow to praise God even before his deliverance comes!

The object of trust is found in the meaning of the Hebrew word "hesed," which God used twice in His answer to Moses' request to "show me Your glory." In the Old Testament, this word hesed is often translated as steadfast love. It is translated as agape in the New Testament. It speaks of God's covenant loyalty. What does this kind of covenant loyalty feel like when it rains down on God's beloved child—me? It feels safe because safety is felt in the loyalty of a powerful presence. And, with the feeling of safety comes praise.

David makes a vow to rejoice when his deliverance comes. Many of the Psalms record references to David keeping his vow to praise God for his deliverances. Too often, we, as the beloved children of God, do not keep our vows to praise Him when we are delivered. We are reminded to keep our vows when we celebrate our deliverances by genuinely worshipping God with praise and gratefulness. This is where worship leading plays a very strategic part in connecting our souls to Him.

I will remember and sing. Singing is not merely about music but about grateful emotion expressed. As David said in the 23rd Psalm, "My cup runneth over." God has engaged me bountifully, and I need be fearful no more. How loyal will I be to what I believe about Him no matter how I feel?

God loves me with a loyal love (hesed), and there is no forgetting. This praise is the fulfillment of an oath, a pledge by David to praise God for his deliverance. Just like David, God will give each of His children a new view of Himself as often as we need one and as often as we ask for one!

This is what a worship leader does! He or she reminds us of God's faithful engagement in our lives, reminds us to complete our vows to be thankful and full of praise, and calls us out to renew our covenant of loyalty when our deliverance comes (again).

Many years ago my wife Falon and I were unexpectedly led by God out of the Nashville Christian music scene, where I was a recording artist and performer, to a mountain town in Northern Arizona. It was in this town where my passion and deep love for the Body of Christ was born. Within a matter of months on staff at a local church, the Lord made very clear to me that I was made to be a worship pastor.

I quickly learned that serving on staff at a church, however, is more difficult than I could have imagined or prepared for. Anyone who has served, whether as a vocational pastor or as a volunteer in the church, can relate and likely agree that this kind of ministry is exhausting and even painful at times.

Within the first couple of years serving in the local church, I realized that there was so much to be done in and for the church community. Due to my adventurous personality and my "fix it and build it" work ethic, I began to take on new roles and responsibilities that were outside the scope of my initial job description. I had developed new leadership skills and, together with some natural talents, found myself really enjoying all of the new and creative outlets that the church allowed me to pursue. So much of this began to fulfill a deep passion in my life. It was so amazing to watch this community of believers grow in their love for Jesus and each other and develop a strong, biblical heart of worship.

What I didn't realize was that through all of this, I had acquired some very unhealthy work habits in my life that began to take root in my heart. I also quickly learned that the leadership style at this church was very much a "let's get the most out of our staff" kind of leadership. I should also mention that our senior pastor had a very strong business model and growth strategy attached to his ministry vision for the team that he was building.

This church soon experienced significant numerical growth and, naturally, the staff and I received a lot of appreciation and support from the church body. This kind of affirmation motivated me to work even harder. It also obligated me to keep thinking outside of the box so that each season could stay relevant and that the momentum would keep building. As the scope of my responsibilities grew, the bar for success kept getting bumped higher and higher. It seemed that every time we turned a new corner, a new ministry need and fresh opportunity presented itself.

At one point, I was developing and pouring into over 75 worship team volunteers and leading 4 worship gatherings each weekend. I was also overseeing the creative arts, the tech team, and the worship interns all while designing and overseeing the graphics and creative communication department. Building and designing grand stage backdrops every time the sermon series changed became my responsibility. I was in charge of writing and recording the church worship projects. I oversaw campus design and aesthetics. Dreaming up and directing the huge annual church events, including what became one of Northern Arizona's largest Christmas Eve festivals, was also on my plate. In addition to all of these responsibilities, I was leading a large young couples small group each week which allowed my wife and I to begin a crisis marriage ministry on the side. Oh yeah, my wife...

Did I mention that, during all of this, I was also working hard to care and provide for my incredibly patient and loving wife as well as our four kids (ALL under the age of five)?

I didn't know I was stressed.
I didn't know what stress was.
I didn't know that I needed rest.
I didn't know what true rest was.

But, then I was reminded of the Good Shepherd from the second verse of Psalm 23: "HE MAKES ME LIE DOWN IN GREEN PASTURES." Because a good and faithful shepherd knows his sheep and what is best for their health and safety,

he knows how to protect them and care for them. I believe that the Lord was "making me lie down." I realized this through a handful of painful experiences and trials.
He made me lie down when I realized that I would come home from work and couldn't keep my eyes open.

He made me lie down when I watched the church staff fall apart and the senior pastor move away.

He made me lie down when the church body struggled and cried out in confusion.

He made me lie down when I realized that I couldn't fix the church or the marriages and relationships that we were pouring into.

He made me lie down when I learned that, due to stress, I had developed shingles on my optic nerve in my right eye and that I would soon go blind.

He made me lie down when I realized that I couldn't remember holding my daughter when she was a baby.

He made me lie down when I found out that my wife struggled to even attend our church because of deep rooted resentment towards those who she perceived were taking advantage of me in leadership.

He made my lie down when my wife told me that she would be happier if I just worked at Starbucks.

He made me lie down when I found out about the miscarriage of our fourth child.

It was in these moments of heartache and discipline that I felt the pressure of my Shepherd's loving hands holding me down, forcing me to rest. I began to understand the fullness of God's patience, mercy, and love.

He broke my will.
He calmed me down.
He pulled me close.
And in the stillness, I heard His voice say:

"My Kingdom and My Church will continue on just fine without you."

I had been working so hard to build what I had thought was God's Kingdom no matter the cost. But, at the end of the day, God exposed my pride and my ego. I was building my own kingdom and sacrificing my health and my family for something that didn't even belong to me!

Through these painful circumstances and struggles, my wife and I found ourselves almost completely burnt out, feeling hopeless and stuck. Even though it would be easier to play the victim and to blame our ministry struggles on church leadership and lack of care and accountability from the elders and church family, I can't. And I won't. I will take the heat and the responsibility on myself because a lot of what I went through was self-inflicted and beautifully God ordained. This is how the Lord led me into a season of repentance and rest. "HE LEADS ME BESIDE QUIET WATERS AND RESTORES MY SOUL."

By God's grace, protection, and faithfulness, He kept my fire for the Church burning bright even though it seemed like everyone and everything was a mess and out of control in the ministry. As my skin thickened and we learned how to properly put on the armor of God, I actually fell deeper in love with our King and His people through the process. Both Falon and I, however, found ourselves wishing that someone would have at least warned us about some of the tests and trials that worship pastors will go through to help us better navigate all of this.

I began to realize that I had been given a certain set of gifts and tools that would eventually lead me to where I am today, leading a ministry called Likewise Worship. In a nutshell, the Lord revealed a deep desire and dream to begin pouring into the next generation of worship pastors that God is preparing. My wife and I are driven to be a preventative and restorative force of encouragement, discipleship, and wisdom for people who have and will experience what we have been through in the church.

In my pursuit to stay focused and aware of where the state of the church was, is presently, and is going to be, I found myself surrounded by a few extremely gifted young leaders that God had strategically put on my path. One of those young men was Josh James, who at the time was a youth group worship leader from Phoenix, Arizona. Within the first few moments of meeting Josh as a 17-year-old high school student, I knew that there was something different and anointed about him. I was on staff during that time as worship pastor at a church in Phoenix, and after developing a mentoring relationship with Josh while still in high school, he soon became a worship intern on my staff.

Over the years of walking alongside Josh on his journey as a young pastor, I had the honor of watching him develop a deep love for God's people and a strong passion for cultivating biblical worship in the church. And now today, through his experiences on a handful of church staffs and ministry education, he has become my right-hand man in building and developing Likewise Worship. Josh's biblical wisdom and maturity go far beyond his age and his grasp of biblical worship in the church is truly compelling and far reaching. Now, I'll let him give you a quick introduction of what you can expect as you read through this book.

Thank you, my friend. The last eight years of my life have been an unexpected adventure. I was raised to know and love the Lord, but I never had a desire or passion for music until junior high.

Through a series of circumstances (including a nasty arm injury), I found myself learning guitar and leading worship.

Though my journey in worship ministry began as a 12-year-old, God's plan and direction for my life didn't really begin to reveal itself until I ended up meeting Justin. Being a worship pastor was never the plan for me growing up, but the Lord was preparing me for ministry years before I even realized it.

Justin played a significant role in helping me discover who God was molding me to be. I share that because one of the biggest reasons that I believe in the ministry of Likewise is because, in many ways, I feel like I am a product of it. Having a wise mentor in my life helped me grow, learn from mistakes, avoid other mistakes, and keep my eyes on Jesus instead of getting wrapped up in myself and my own identity. And, I am so grateful!

The contents of this book are simply a collection of beliefs, thoughts, and reflections about worship leadership that we have learned along the way. Our greatest influences upon these conclusions are, first and foremost, the Word of God, and, secondly, our own trials, hardships, and experiences.

We believe wholeheartedly that God's Word is a "lamp to our feet and a light to our path" (Ps. 119:5), not only in our daily lives, but also in how we think about the ministry we do. So, it has always been our commitment to, with a pure heart, understand how to best serve God's people in a way that is consistent with Scripture to the best of our understanding.

In terms of our experiences, both of us have endured hardship and some brokenness during our walks in ministry. You'll hear some of those stories woven throughout the book. We have found, however, that these difficult times have been the times where the Lord has taught us the most and where we have learned to depend upon Him.

As you read this, we want you to know a few things:

- This book is not a "one size fits all" prescription for worship leading. Inside this book you will find suggested "principles" to be applied. We encourage the worship pastor to apply these principles in a way that makes sense in their own community.

- We don't believe we have all of the answers. This book is an expression of what we have come to learn and believe throughout the years. And, because we have seen fruit in leading this way, we want to share what the Lord has done in our lives and ministries.

- The "principles" found in this book do not fit one "style" of music. Whether your church sings only contemporary songs, Gospel, or hymns, etc., we believe these principles can be helpful.

- We do not advocate for a specific "style" of music, either. We want worship pastors to understand the people in their communities and decide how to lead based on who they are leading and not any cultural pressure.

- We LOVE the local church and believe in God's purposes for it. Our mission as worship leaders is to unite the Body of Christ around the truths of the Gospel by singing them! As long as the Body is divided, the work of The Church will be hindered.

- If you are an aspiring worship pastor, we hope this opens your eyes to all that goes into this pastoral role. And, through that, we pray that God gives you clarity and wisdom as you pursue your gifts and calling.

- Lastly, this book is not just a "how-to." The heart of the Likewise Worship ministry is to care for and disciple worship pastors. What we mean by "care for" and "disciple" is that it is our greatest aim to provide a space for worship pastors to experience authentic community and, within that community, help worship pastors follow Jesus and obey His commands. If you're a worship pastor reading this, we would love to go on this journey with you!

YOU ARE A "PASTOR"

WORSHIP PASTOR = Shepherd, Humble Servant, Leader, Unifier, Protector, Minister, Sheepdog, Disciple, Friend.

DEFINITION:
The word "PASTOR" is a Latin noun, which means "SHEPHERD" and is derived from the verb pascere – "to lead to pasture, set to grazing, cause to eat".[1]

We share this definition and other descriptors of a "pastor" with you up front, mainly because throughout this book you will hear us refer to today's worship and music leaders or ministers as "worship pastors." We believe it is important to help establish a sense of gravity and authority to this role in the church. We also strongly believe that for someone to fully grasp the basic role of a "pastor" in the local church, there must be first a heart of humility and a deep desire to be a servant of others.

One of my mentors once suggested to me that the church has a humility crisis. He explained it this way: "true biblical humility starts with being suspicious about your own heart first." This should lead us to ask these questions about ourselves: What does the word of God reveal about me and my life? What is the Holy Spirit exposing in my own heart? When we focus most of our attention on what the Lord is doing in our own hearts, we will be able to better imitate the humility and servanthood of Jesus in our relationships and ministries.

At Likewise Worship, we strongly believe it is important to avoid quickly slapping authoritative titles on certain leadership roles in the church, especially when the individual carrying the title might not be ready or qualified to uphold the weight and responsibility. We do, however, believe that the worship and music leader role in the local church needs to be seen and acknowledged simply for what it is: a shepherding and pastoral position. There is really no way around this, especially when it comes to how the majority of the sheep that we are leading naturally perceive this role.

It is important to us as a ministry to make sure all of our worship pastors understand the burden they carry when they step on to the church stage to shepherd God's people in a time of worship through corporate singing. Regardless of their education, training, or experience, it is imperative that this position is seen as highly influential and impactful on the body as a whole. When these musically gifted individuals fully understand how important their role is to the unity of the body, it makes for a heightened sense of personal accountability and responsibility in their hearts for what they are called to do before God.

Overall, we make it a point not to get hung up on certain titles in the church as this can become quite divisive. We simply believe that as disciples of Jesus Himself, we all have this common responsibility to imitate Christ and to live out the gospel in all that we say and do. What an honor and privilege to serve in the Kingdom of our Creator!

GO AND DO LIKEWISE

Jesus commissioned a handful of radical followers to lead His church. They woke up everyday with an urgency for the gospel, knowing that their time is short and that the sheep will scatter without strong, shepherding leadership. Encouraged by the example set by these leaders who have gone before us, Josh and I are driven to go and DO LIKEWISE as we come alongside today's worship pastors.

We cannot overemphasize the fact that there is NOT a "one size fits all" model for worship in the Church today. But, it is our prayer that the biblical wisdom, stories, experiences, and philosophical direction that you read in these ten chapters will inspire and minister to your heart and impact the way you lead God's people.

Thank you for serving the Lord and for allowing us to share what we have learned on our ministry journeys with you. You are loved and you are not alone!

-- Justin Unger & Josh James

CHAPTER 1

The Shepherd & HIS Sheep

What does it mean to be a pastor? What does it mean to be in "full-time ministry?" What is a worship pastor's role or primary responsibility? Why does it matter? Those seem like questions we know the answers to, or at least should know the answers to. But, if we are being honest, in today's culture, it is not uncommon to just all of a sudden be "doing ministry" or "leading worship." While there's not a "right" way to enter into ministry, I think it is worthwhile to pause and consider the ministry to which God has called us. Because, if we don't, then we could just be building our own kingdoms without even knowing it.

So let's unpack this.

Throughout Scripture, we are introduced to many shepherds, both literal and metaphorical. The basic role of a shepherd is to care for their flock. Under this umbrella of care is the responsibility to protect the sheep from danger as well as to lead them to a place where they can rest, eat, and drink. Understanding the dynamic between a shepherd and his flock is a good place to start as we attempt to answer these questions about what exactly it is we are called to do.

Culturally, pastors are often referred to as "shepherds" of people. While that is a helpful way of understanding our role, it tempts us to forget that we are first sheep of the Good Shepherd, Jesus (John 10:1-18). Peter referred to Jesus as the "Chief Shepherd" when laying out the roles of the Overseers of the church (1 Peter 5:2-4). In Psalm 23, David acknowledges God as his shepherd. In order to grasp what it means to care for others emotionally and spiritually, we must start by observing the life of Jesus.

THE GOOD SHEPHERD

As the Good Shepherd, Jesus was a protector of people. He didn't protect people with violence or wield any weapon. He protected their dignity and humanity with the truth about the Kingdom. Jesus was a pursuer of people. Jesus was patient with His disciples as they struggled to understand who He was and the significance of His identity. Jesus was the feet-washing servant who set an example by how He lived. Jesus laid down His life for the sheep. He described Himself in this way:

"I am the good shepherd. The good shepherd lays down his life for the sheep. He who is a hired hand and not a shepherd, who does not own the sheep, sees the wolf coming and leaves the sheep and flees, and the wolf snatches them and scatters them. He flees because he is a hired hand and cares nothing for the sheep. I am the good shepherd. I know my own and my own know me, just as the Father knows me and I know the Father; and I lay down my life for the sheep." - John 10:11-15

This is who a shepherd is. This is what a shepherd does. As disciples of Jesus, this is how we should think about caring for those we lead.

But since we, too, are sheep, it would be helpful to understand ourselves in relation to our Good Shepherd.

ALL WE LIKE SHEEP

There are conflicting opinions about the nature of sheep. But, what I think everyone can agree on is that sheep are naturally dependent followers. They tend to stray and wander without adequate direction. The prophet Isaiah even used sheep as a way to illustrate how we have wandered from The Lord: "All we like sheep have gone astray; we have turned - every one - to his own way" (Is. 53:6).

It seems to me that sheep aren't stupid but are rather innocent, submissive, and meek. How many times have you read a news story about a sheep attack? Or a sheep mutiny after the shepherd has disciplined or corrected one of the flock?

While we as people can find ourselves to be a little more reactionary and violent than sheep (unfortunately), we have the same basic tendency to be followers. What I mean by this is that deep down, we all desire to identify the "right way" or the "right path." What often defines us and changes the trajectory of our lives is what or whom we decide to follow.

Consider this real life article first published by USA Today in 2005:

"First one sheep jumped to its death. Then stunned Turkish shepherds, who had left the herd to graze while they had breakfast, watched as nearly 1,500 others followed, each leaping off the same cliff, Turkish media reported.
In the end, 450 dead animals lay on top of one another in a billowy white pile, the Aksam newspaper said. Those who jumped later were saved as the pile got higher and the fall more cushioned, Aksam reported."[2]

JESUS DOESN'T LEAVE US TO FIGURE IT ALL OUT. AS THE GOOD SHEPHERD, HE TELLS US THAT HE KNOWS THE WAY. HE IS THE WAY.

You can laugh at that. But not too hard, because this mishap actually cost these poor families about $100,000. The point is no one really knows why the first sheep jumped, including all of the sheep that jumped after it. Yet, somehow 1,500 sheep followed one another off of a cliff. If our attention is not on our Shepherd, we have this tendency to follow after whatever or whoever promises to lead us or show us the "way."

But, Jesus doesn't leave us to figure it all out. As the Good Shepherd, He tells us that He knows the way. He IS the way (John 14:6). If Jesus is the way, that means I am not the way. Your senior pastor is not the way. You are not the way. He invites us to follow Him.

Now may be a good time to pause and reflect on that. Your purpose as a worship pastor is not to be a trailblazer, forging your own untrodden path of new experiences and ideas. Your purpose is to use your gift and influence to help people follow the way of Jesus.

Creativity? All for it.

Programs? All for them.

New original worship songs? All for them.

But the arrows of all of your creative and visionary thinking should be aimed at one thing: helping others follow the way of Jesus of Nazareth.

So if we already have a Shepherd, then are we just wannabes? More mature sheep? Gifted sheep? Or is this analogy breaking down in front of our eyes? We'll let our 21st-century shepherd friend help us out.

SHEEPDOGS

One year I was driving home from a camping trip with my family in Greer, Arizona. As we drove, I noticed something

along the left side of the highway that forced me to pull over, take in the beauty, and turn it into a teaching moment for my family and I. In the distance, I saw a giant gray colored cloud-like blob moving down the side of a large green hill. When I realized what I was seeing, I had to dash across the highway to get a closer look. Sure enough, this gray blob was a huge flock of sheep. I watched hundreds of sheep stay close together as they made their way down the hillside towards this pond of water for a drink on a hot day. I started to wonder, what was keeping them together in a unified group? There was no shepherd in sight and my curiosity turned into confusion knowing that sheep are not naturally good at staying together on their own. Then, I looked closer and noticed a few dozen sheepdogs surrounding the parameter of the flock. These sheepdogs were clearly leading them on their journey and keeping them in line with one another. There were even a few moments when one of the sheep would wander outside of the rest and the dogs would chase it down and lead it back into the group by nipping at its ankles. It was such a cool visual. It provided a moment for me to ponder the role of the sheepdogs and before I knew it, over the hill I saw the shepherd coming on a quad with staff in hand. It made perfect sense as I thought about how the sheepdogs clearly knew the will and direction of the shepherd as they led the sheep to the water. It really helped me put in perspective my humble role as one of the Lord's sheepdogs. As a pastor, it is my role to keep the unity of the body and to work together with the other sheepdogs to lead, protect, feed, and care for the sheep on this journey. **Even though the thought of being considered a "dog" in ministry is not that appealing, it is an honor to be appointed by the Chief Shepherd to care for His sheep in whatever capacity.**

Now we are coming into focus! Sheepdogs have been the most helpful way of understanding our roles in ministry. Let's talk about them.

First, sheepdogs are bred and trained. There are different breeds of sheepdogs with unique skill sets. Shepherds will use certain sheepdogs based on their environments and potential predators.

However, most sheepdogs are expected to perform four basic duties: mustering, herding, droving, and guarding the livestock.

Mustering is a duty of the sheepdog for the purpose of gathering all of the sheep into a group so that they travel together as a unit.

Herding is the process of moving this group of sheep from one place to another (maybe from watering hole to feeding area).

Droving is a lot like herding but happens over a much longer distance (think town to town or hillside to hillside). There are different tactics used by sheepdogs for droving than herding. Like nipping at the legs of the sheep as they begin to wander from the flock.

And finally, the sheepdogs protect the sheep from potential dangers and predators.

Together, these are insightful. The fundamental job of the sheepdog is twofold. One, to know exactly where the shepherd wants to go and to help the sheep arrive at his intended destination. This requires the sheepdog to be intimately familiar with the ways and desires of the shepherd. Two, to protect the sheep from wandering off and to guard them from the things that wish to destroy them.

We are sheepdogs. Every time we gather together with those in our communities, it is our job to help them be unified. It is our job to lead them from the chaos of their week with its competing agendas to the clarity and green pastures of intentional communion with God. His intended destination for all of us is obedience and trust. It is our job to not view church as an event, but rather as a family. It is our job to walk alongside these people on the pilgrimage of what Eugene Peterson understood from those who have gone before him as a "long obedience in the same direction."[3] It is our job to help protect them from wandering.

DIFFERENT TYPES OF SHEEP

In order to perform these duties well, we must not only know the Shepherd intimately, but also have a knowledge of those we are leading. In any given community, there are most likely

four different types of sheep, or churchgoers: lost, lean, fat, and healthy.

Lost Sheep

These precious little sheep are wandering in the darkness, lost and afraid. They are confused and unaware of who they are and why they exist. They are often found stuck in traps and in chains, longing to be rescued and yearning to hear the peaceful voice of the Shepherd for direction and purpose. They have yet to understand true love and have never experienced true rest.

Lean Sheep

These little ones are malnourished. They are hungry, but they don't feel completely satisfied or filled. They tend to rebel often and wander outside of the fold in search of their identity and sense of belonging. They desire direction and guidance from the Shepherd but often find themselves outside of His will, leaning on their own plans and being controlled by their feelings. They love the taste of "warm milk" but have not yet enjoyed a healthy meal to help them to grow stronger. They are comforted by the voice of the Shepherd but quickly fall into doubt and mistrust. They try to stay close by the Shepherd but are prone to distraction and wandering. In the Church, they enjoy following those around them and feeding off of the scraps and leftovers at times. They try to get connected by serving but they struggle with commitment. The lean sheep have a strong future and so much potential.

Fat Sheep

These poor overweight sheep are comfortable and lazy. They are slow and in the way. Constantly consuming, they find themselves concerned only about what they are being fed and how it is being fed to them. They know the Shepherd's voice but have a hard time hearing Him over their own voice and other noises. They are quickly annoyed and impatient with the other sheep and are quick to push the young and weak ones out of their way.

In the Church, the fat sheep are quick to whine and complain about changes. They are mostly worried about how any change will affect themselves. They give and serve at times but never until it hurts and often for status, or to be seen. They are slow to invite outsiders into their circle of influence and are quick to push out anyone that stands in their way. The fat sheep have a distorted view of worship in the Church and make their preferences and negative opinions known to many for the purpose of gaining influence and swaying leadership. They are consumed by fear and pride. They lack joy and encouragement. They have forgotten their first love, their passion for discipleship, and their urgency to reach the lost.

Healthy Sheep

These sheep are visibly healthy and happy. They are completely dependent not on themselves but on the Shepherd. They are clearly filled with joy and strength as they are full of energy and excitement, living with confidence in the moment, and rejoicing and resting in the presence of the Good Shepherd. The healthy sheep are filled with grace, peace, and humility as they have been broken and carried by the Shepherd along the way. They are not worried about the road ahead or concerned about where or when their next meal will come. They find daily comfort and restoration by quiet waters when they are thirsty. They can clearly discern the voice of the Shepherd above all the other voices and noises around them.

In the Church, the healthy sheep come alongside the lean sheep and the fat sheep with patience, understanding, and grace. They sacrifice their own provisions

IN ORDER TO PERFORM THESE DUTIES WELL, WE MUST NOT ONLY KNOW THE SHEPHERD INTIMATELY, BUT ALSO HAVE A KNOWLEDGE OF THOSE WE ARE LEADING.

to take care of those in need. They thrive when things are uncomfortable and are relaxed when things change. They are always finding new ways to serve in the Church and are committed to building up the body. Their hearts break for the lost sheep, and they will do whatever it takes to reach them.

Knowing your community is essential to leading it well. There will be people all across this spectrum, and they will find themselves in different places from season to season. But, an awareness of your own heart as well as others' is crucial to leading well.

THE SHEEP FILTER

So much of our mission as we encourage ministry leaders to "go and do likewise" is to funnel everything through what we like to call the "Sheep Filter". The Sheep Filter is the lens by which we see those that we are leading. The Sheep Filter allows us to understand those that have been placed in our care and reminds us that all that we do should be done with them in mind. This is part of how we fulfill Jesus' charge to His disciple Peter in John 21:15-17, to:

a) **Feed My Sheep**
b) **Tend My Flock**
c) **Take Care of My Lambs**

We have to grasp this heavy burden that Jesus has for HIS sheep and make sure that we are up for the challenge of doing what it takes to fulfill the same charge that He gave to Peter. It is in response to our love for Jesus that we put His sheep before ourselves as we lead them and care for them. The "Sheep Filter" must be on our minds as we work through the rest of these chapters together.

Acts 20:28 - Pay careful attention to yourselves and to all the flock, in which the Holy Spirit has made you overseers, to care for the church of God, which he obtained with his own blood.

1 Peter 5:2 - Shepherd the flock of God that is among you, exercising oversight, not under compulsion, but willingly, as God would have you; not for shameful gain, but eagerly;

THE REST OF THIS BOOK

The rest of this book talks about how we do these things more practically. But what must be noted is that it is ultimately the Lord who accomplishes everything. Paul put it this way:

"For when one says, "I follow Paul," and another, "I follow Apollos," are you not being merely human? What then is Apollos? What is Paul? Servants through whom you believed, as the Lord assigned to each. I planted, Apollos watered, but God gave the growth. So neither he who plants nor he who waters is anything, but only God who gives the growth. He who plants and he who waters are one, and each will receive his wages according to his labor. For we are God's fellow workers. You are God's field, God's building." - 1 Corinthians 3:4-9

All of the work we do is seed-sowing and soil-tilling. God takes what we give Him and makes something out of it. So, this means that the pressure is off of you to be responsible for anyone's growth in discipleship. All God asks us to do is to know Him, be faithful to Him, and join Him in His work. That is one of the greatest invitations and blessings of all.

The reality is that we live in a world desperate for meaning and purpose. Each day we are bombarded with messages and images describing the "good life." There is a better way. We all just need the invitation.

CHAPTER 2

The Gathering of the Saints

In the first chapter, we looked at our lives in relation to Jesus in order to determine our roles as worship pastors. We remembered that we are, first, sheep who belong to the Good Shepherd. Although we have been called to "shepherd" God's people, it is ultimately Jesus who charts the course for us. Our goal is to help people follow His way, not our own. And the best way to understand our role is to look at the sheepdog. Under the Chief Shepherd's guidance and direction, we are to lead God's people to His desired destination.

In this chapter, we aim to understand why it is important for followers of Jesus to gather together regularly. The authors of Scripture understood that meeting together, praying together, eating together, and especially singing together were of incredible importance. Our task is to steward these gatherings in such a way that their intended impact (of unity in the body and the true worship of God) is felt and experienced as much as possible.

The gathering of the saints is such a beautiful gift from God that is intended to unite us together, to help us remember the truths of Scripture, to encourage us, equip us, and to send us out into the world to do the work of the gospel. What we have learned about the local church in America, however, is that the very thing that was created and designed by God to unite His people has been hijacked and manipulated by the enemy to divide God's people. This is alarming because we have been given the Spirit of God and the Word of God to discern the schemes of the enemy, yet we often ignore and minimize the effects that these divisions have on the Body of Christ as a whole.

Before we go further into the purpose of the gathering, let us consider a few basic truths about what worship is, according to Scripture.

WHY WORSHIP?

One of the first references to worship in the bible is found in the book of Genesis when Cain and Abel both brought an offering to the Lord (Genesis 4). The Lord was clearly satisfied with the worship and sacrifice of Abel, but had no regard for Cain's. We read that although Cain did bring an offering, it was Abel who brought the best of what he had: the firstborn of his flock. What was revealed about the heart and motives of Abel through his sacrifice was that he desired to give his best to God, no matter the cost. This kind of worship exemplifies an acceptable sacrifice to the Lord. And, in Romans 12 we can clearly see what a biblical sacrifice of worship truly looks like.

Therefore I urge you, brethren, by the mercies of God, to present your bodies a living and holy sacrifice, acceptable to God, which is your spiritual service of worship. And do not be conformed to this world, but be transformed by the renewing of your mind, so that you may prove what the will of God is, that which is good and acceptable and perfect. For through the grace given to me I say to everyone among you not to think more highly of himself than he ought to think; but to think so as to have sound judgment, as God has allotted to each a measure of faith. For just as we have many members in one body and all the members do not have the same function, so we, who are many, are one body in Christ, and individually members one of another. - Romans 12:1-5

According to this passage, true worship requires a holy sacrifice which is our spiritual service. We find in Hebrews the same theme when it says, "Through Him then let us continually offer up a sacrifice of praise to God, that is, the fruit of lips that acknowledge His name" (Heb. 13:15).

This truth requires us to lay down our "personal preferences" and become more like Christ as we first look to the interests of others.

John Piper echoes the heart of Romans 12 this way:

"God wants visible, lived-out, bodily evidence that our lives are built on His mercy. Just as worshipers in the Old Testament denied themselves some earthly treasure (a sheep, a goat, a bull) and carried their sacrifices to the altar of blood and fire, so we deny ourselves some earthly treasure or ease or comfort, and carry ourselves — our bodies — for Christ's sake to the places and the relationships and the crises in this world where mercy is needed."[4]

So, a couple of things should be clear to us:

1. Worship is not just music and singing. Worship encompasses our giving, our obedience, our entire lives. Worship happens when we use any aspect of our lives to express that we believe God to be of more worth than anything in the world.

2. The worship of God costs us something. For some, it is time. For others, it is physical resources or pleasures. And for many of us in today's culture, worshipping together may require us to sacrifice our musical preference.

THE "GATHERING" PURPOSE

Throughout Scripture, we find specific purposes for gathering and singing together. And the heart behind these examples is seen in Jesus' prayer for us in John 17.

Before Jesus left for the Garden of Gethsemane with His disciples, to eventually be betrayed and arrested, he prayed. He prayed not only for His disciples but also for those who would "believe in me through their word" (17:20). We fall under that category. Jesus prayed for us.

And what is most interesting about this prayer is the one specific thing Jesus prayed for regarding us: "that they may all be one, just as you, Father, are in me, and I in you, that they also may be in us, so that the world may believe that you have sent me" (17:21).

THE WORSHIP OF GOD COSTS US SOMETHING.

Of all things Jesus could have prayed for, He prayed that we would be unified! For He knew that when we are unified, the world would believe in Him.

Gathering together, praying together, eating together, singing together… all of it was meant to give glory to God and unify His people.

The author of Hebrews wrote this about meeting together: "And let us consider how to stir up one another to love and good works, not neglecting to meet together, as is the habit of some, but encouraging one another, and all the more as you see the Day drawing near" (10:24-25).

This was written to a people enduring opposition and persecution. The encouragement was to not give up meeting together because we need each other! We need each other to press on to the end.

A COMMAND TO SING TOGETHER

Singing together is an essential part of this "pressing on." Jesus sang with His disciples on the Mount of Olives before they went to Gethsemane (Matthew 26:30). What an example of singing to press on, singing to encourage.

Paul knew the impact and importance of singing better than many. In Colossians 3, Paul tells the church that they have new life solely because of what Christ did for them, not their own work (3:1-4). And from this security in Christ's work, they were to put to death the evil things inside them (3:5-11). And then, Paul gives a suggestion on how to accomplish this:

"And let the peace of Christ rule in your hearts, to which indeed you were called in one body. And be thankful. Let the word of Christ dwell in you richly, teaching and admonishing one another in all wisdom, singing psalms and hymns and spiritual songs, with thankfulness in your hearts to God." (3:15-17).

To Paul, singing psalms, hymns, and spiritual songs together was one of the main ways we can let the word of Christ dwell in us.

We sing together to give praise to God. To adore Him. To lift Him high. But we also sing to remember. We remember truths about Him and His character. We remember that we are under His care. We remember His faithfulness to past generations.

In Psalm 77, Asaph questions the goodness, faithfulness, care, and compassion of God. And then, he sings:

"I will remember the deeds of the Lord; yes, I will remember your wonders of old. I will ponder all your work, and meditate on your mighty deeds. Your way, O God, is holy. What god is great like our God?" (77:11-13).

In a time of despair and desperation, the psalmist sings to remind himself (and others, as this was to be sung in the congregation) that God has proven Himself faithful time and time again.

Singing together is a way for us to remember the character of God and the big story we are a part of. It helps us keep a big view of God. He is the great and faithful King who always delivers His people.

Lifting our voices together also lifts our hearts up in faith. I can remember a time on my college campus when I attended a worship service and didn't feel like singing. It was one of those difficult seasons where I just didn't feel like I had a song to lift up. So, I stood there, surrounded by the voices of other believers. As I heard their collective voice, something happened in my heart. I wanted to sing again. I believe that God was using the faith of others, expressed in singing, to light my own present darkness.

When we come to sing together, we don't just come to get a "spiritual fix." We come to give God glory and to encourage our neighbor with our voices.

But, what if you don't feel like it? Does that mean you are being fake? Or that the worship isn't real? That is an honest question.

Eugene Peterson writes this in response:

We live in what is called… "the age of sensation." We think that if we don't feel something then there can be no authenticity in doing it. But the wisdom of God says something different: that we can act ourselves into a new way of feeling much quicker than we can feel ourselves into a new way of acting. Worship is an act that develops feelings for God… When we obey the command to praise God in worship, our deep, essential need to be in relationship with God is nurtured.[5]

We lift our voices for God and we lift our voices for our neighbors.

As a worship pastor, I have learned that there is one thing that is arguably the most unifying piece of our worship gathering as a church: singing together. Singing together is commanded by God for the purpose of unity, encouragement, and admonishment.

IF WE LEAD WORSHIP WITH OUR OWN INTERESTS AND DESIRES IN MIND, WE WILL MISS THE OPPORTUNITY TO MINISTER TO A LARGE PORTION OF OUR CONGREGATIONS.

There is something supernatural about singing together that has united humans throughout the history of the world. And, this experience is not limited just to "worship" songs. You can

go to a big concert and the minute you begin singing those familiar lyrics with the vast crowd of fans, you feel connected to them and cannot explain why. It is a universal language created by God that binds us together and when it is used for His purposes and glory, it fulfills His will for us.

This is why we are commanded to sing. There are so many believers that do not take this command seriously. They are so hung up on their preferences, or they will show up late, or even wait outside the door for the music to end.

It is no wonder the enemy uses music in thousands of churches all across America as a divisive tool.

These contentious divisions have even been called "worship wars." Music style, song choices, song arrangements, and lyrics are all examples of this. Notice in the Colossians passage that Paul describes three types of songs he encouraged: psalms, hymns, and spiritual songs. All different types of songs are important and fulfill the divine purpose to unite us. As a worship pastor, it has been so hard to witness the division caused by musical preference in churches all across the country.

SWIMMING UPSTREAM

One of the greatest challenges we face as leaders in our culture is that to deny oneself for the greater good is to swim upstream. Almost everything around us informs our cultural posture as consumers. In that light, it is not all that surprising that we are tempted to treat church the way we treat the mall or the market.

However, this should not be so. And it takes leadership from the front and discipleship along the way to correct course.

So, we must first look at ourselves. Are we driven by our preferences? Do we lead only songs that we like, or that resonate with us? Do we lead songs that we do not like? Are we willing to, as we discussed in the previous chapter, take a long look at who we are leading and use that as the filter through which we make decisions?

If we lead worship with our own interests and desires in mind, we will miss the opportunity to minister to a large portion of our congregations.

For example, if I lead worship at a youth camp, would it make sense for me to sing a lot of hymns that they would not know? Or, if I were to find myself leading a congregation that mostly knew the old hymns, would it make sense to sing four songs off of the newest record?

Good leaders are willing to shelve their own preferences, if necessary, to lead appropriately in their context.

And let the peace of Christ rule in your hearts, to which indeed you were called in one body. And be thankful. Let the word of Christ dwell in you richly, teaching and admonishing one another in all wisdom, singing psalms and hymns and spiritual songs, with thankfulness in your hearts to God.

COLOSSIANS 3:15-17

CHAPTER 3

Practical Practices

In addition to laying aside our own preferences, there are some other helpful aspects of worship leading to be mindful of. Much of the content in this book is "philosophical" in nature. So, before we do our deep dive into that, we wanted to share some thoughts about how we physically lead from the stage in a helpful way.

IT IS NOT ABOUT YOU AND HOW YOU WORSHIP.

As we make certain sacrifices as the worship pastor, we are putting on display the very thing that we desire the sheep to do when they gather together. So now, back to the concept of the sheep filter! If we, as worship pastors, are focused first on the health and unity of these sheep, then we need to make sure that as we lead them, they know that we love them and can clearly see them. Literally, SEE them!

EYE CONTACT

Leading music from the stage can be intimidating at times and can put to test our confidence in who we are and what we are made to do. One of the ways we see a lot of worship leaders cope with this lack of confidence is by closing their eyes. We fool ourselves into thinking that if we can't see them, they can't see us. This allows us to feel more comfortable when it seems like there is little engagement. It even allows us to appear more worshipful. But, we have learned that the sheep need our eye contact. They need to see that we see them. They also need to see that we are confident in our leadership of them. Eye contact is one of the best ways we can lead with honesty and vulnerability.

WE NEED TO LEARN TO STOP OVERTHINKING THE PERFORMANCE SIDE OF OUR CALLING AS WORSHIP PASTORS.

Oftentimes, as I look across the room and lock eyes with certain people, I find that eye contact breaks down walls and creates an opportunity for me to specifically minister to that person for a moment. This can happen through the lyrics of the song or the smile on my face that shows them that I care for them. Sometimes, I will notice someone (usually a man) that is not singing and, when we lock eyes, that person begins to sing again. Remember, the sheep are constantly distracted and prone to wander even in the middle of a song or service. All of this may require you to be more prepared as a leader. Being prepared allows you to open your eyes, take them off of the confidence monitor, and lift them up from your music stand. It is impossible to engage the people you are leading if your eyes are glued to your music stand! They need confident and humble leaders to keep them connected to the Lord and to each other.

SELF-FOCUSED WORSHIP

The reality is that it is very difficult to lead well if we are focused inwardly. Some people may be moved to worship by your expression of worship, but that doesn't equal good worship leadership. Remember, this time for corporate worship is not your personal worship time. There should be many moments throughout the week where it is just "you and the Lord." And the way you lead on the weekend should be influenced by those intimate times! But when it comes to the corporate gathering, your job is to help others sing together. And this requires you to engage them and walk alongside them as they learn to participate.

This also requires you to examine your expression. Here is a good question to always ask yourself: is what I am about to do going to help or hinder someone's participation? This should be applied to song selection, what you say in the middle of service, how you move about on stage, and every other aspect of worship leadership. The measure of success for your leadership is that people are united in singing the truth together.

SPIRIT LED OR CANNED?

Sometimes what we say before, after, or even in the middle of a song can really do a lot of good to help bring the lyrics we are singing into focus. I love the opportunity to speak into the messages of some of the songs and even read scripture that might enhance our personal connection with the lyrics. It is important, however, that we be sensitive and self-controlled as this can also become a distraction and be over the top. Remember, the songs themselves have so much to teach us and remind us. Less is more in this area.

As we discussed in a previous chapter, sheep are not stupid. Most of them can pick up on counterfeit passion and superficial emotion. This can tear apart trust and quickly come off as a performance if we are not careful. For instance, I have heard worship leaders stop to pray or say something before a song and suddenly, in that moment, they have supernaturally acquired an English accent! I have also noticed that sometimes there are cliche things to say in our song transitions or our call to worship (things learned from a Youtube worship video) that come across forced or canned. We need to learn to stop overthinking the performance side of our calling as worship pastors. The Church loves heartfelt vulnerability even if it is not fully polished like the worship artists out there.

SUNDAY RECALIBRATION

Sunday morning is a time for recalibration. Gathering together points our compass back to "true north." It is the time when the church comes together to sing, listen, pray, and take communion (among other things).

All of these things are a means by which we learn to love God rather than other things.

This recalibration of our hearts is accomplished through repetition and storytelling. Immersing ourselves in the complete, true story of the world (creation, fall, redemption, restoration) through repetition causes us to keep a high view of God.

Part of our role in this is to do everything in our power to to help people participate in the storytelling. As we will see, even the tiniest distraction can keep people from being engaged.

CHAPTER 4

The Worship Service & Flow

Now that we have considered some of the biblical, practical, and philosophical reasons for the gathering of the saints, and practical "do's and dont's", let's discuss how we can put it all together.

Many American churches struggle with their Sunday gatherings when it comes to the service flow and experience. The service flow is often disrupted and the purpose of the gathering is confused when church leaders fail to be intentionally creative and sensitive to the leading of the Spirit. What if our Sunday gatherings were simple and seamless from beginning to end for the purpose of capturing and keeping the attention of the distracted sheep?

We all are familiar with different "types" of churches. Lutheran, Methodist, Non-Denominational, Pentecostal, Catholic, and the list goes on. What is unique to these different traditions is not only theology, but also "liturgy."

If you grew up in more of a "high church" or Catholic setting, you may be more familiar with this term. Liturgy, or the liturgical church, can carry all sorts of connotations. For some, it is the tradition they are trying to escape. For others, it is the structure that they crave. In any case, we must be aware of the "liturgy" of our churches.

For starters, liturgy just means form, or formula. It was the prescribed way by which a church worshipped. Liturgy often includes Scripture, communion, praying, reading, symbols, and other elements. Some believe that liturgy is stale and lifeless--that it is just ritualistic box-checking. And it can be, but so could any religious act or gathering. But, I believe that thoughtful liturgy is an opportunity. Each church has a liturgy. But what thoughtful liturgy does so well is help you tell the story.

This is important because storytelling is at the heart of our corporate gatherings. Our time to meet together is our time to recalibrate our hearts towards God and remember the bigger story that we are a part of. And the way that we tell the story and the elements we use matter.

THE FILM SCORE

When you watch your favorite movie you will quickly see that the director of the film desires to keep your complete attention the entire time by weaving in musical transitions and

emotional scenes without distractions from the storyline. The director knows that if there is even one point of disconnect they could lose their intended audience to the more engaging things in life. We are so easily distracted by smartphones, work issues, school deadlines, and other busybody things.

OUR TIME TO MEET TOGETHER IS OUR TIME TO RECALIBRATE OUR HEARTS TOWARDS GOD AND REMEMBER THE BIGGER STORY THAT WE ARE A PART OF.

You are the director of the Sunday gathering "movie score." You must take ownership of the service and find ways to use every element of the service to tell the Gospel story in an engaging way.

THE WORSHIP PASTOR / CONDUCTOR

It is our job to take command of every moving piece of a service. From the moment the worship center doors open to the closing prayer or benediction, we must intentionally have a firm grasp on each transition and element. This is why we encourage and recommend a "simple service" approach. The more things you add to the service, the harder it is to execute everything well and limit distractions.

Managing and directing all of the people involved in the service with a humble, yet confident heart is the goal. Everyone involved needs to see that you care about them and their part in the service while you hold the reigns. We encourage you to consider scheduling a pre-service meeting each week inviting everyone who is involved in that service from the ushers and greeters to the musicians and speakers. This will allow you to share your vision for the transitions in the service and keep everyone "in the know." Take the time to make sure that everyone who has a role in the service is prepared to execute their role effectively.

SIMPLE SERVICE

Simplicity promotes quality. We often overthink the flow of our worship services, filling them with nice but often pointless gestures that most of the church body forgets about by the time they leave the building.

What if this one hour that we have together was intentionally simple and to the point? We should always be thinking about the "why" behind every element in the service. It is helpful to think about everything you do in a service and if you do not have a good reason for why you do something, maybe it is time to rethink that element of the service.

SIMPLICITY PROMOTES QUALITY. WE SHOULD ALWAYS BE THINKING ABOUT THE "WHY" BEHIND EVERY ELEMENT IN THE SERVICE.

Different emphasis is placed on different service elements depending upon the church and community you are leading. So, it is important to be sensitive to these things while considering how you can enhance or simplify them. Find a way to get everything to make sense.

THE CALL TO WORSHIP

The call to worship is far different from a "welcome." While it may include that, the purpose of the call to worship is to communicate to everyone gathered that we are in the presence of God and we have come to worship Him. It is the point at which you use whatever method of choice to communicate that it is time to collectively place all of our attention upon God.

There are many different creative ways of doing this. But, the call to worship should set the stage for the rest of the gathering. Calls to worship are generally reverent, acknowledging the otherness of God and His worthiness of our attention and affection. Calls to worship should remind us that God is big! Calls to worship should prepare our hearts to give God our songs and prayers.

Here are a few ideas for an engaging Call to Worship:

Corporate Scripture Reading

The reading of God's Word together is powerful. You may have someone read a passage of Scripture over the congregation. It is also helpful to put a passage of Scripture on the screen and have the congregation read it aloud together. This really promotes participation, engagement, and attention.

Here are a few helpful Call to Worship passages:

Psalm 47:1-2
Psalm 95:1-3; 6-7
Psalm 96:1-4
Psalm 100

There are countless passages we can use. And, they do not have to be Psalms. Any text that encourages people to lift their songs and cast their burdens will work great!

When it comes to the reading of Scripture as a call to worship, it is helpful to make sure that the reading is not too long. If the reading is lengthy, then there is a greater chance that the congregation will not grasp what the passage is communicating and thereby miss its intended purpose.

Choosing passages that focus on God's greatness and God's care for us as His people are generally powerful verses to use during these times.

Opening Prayer

It is often helpful to use prayer as a call to worship. As we have mentioned, we can be easily distracted. This would be an appropriate time to pray for that very thing, that God would give us eyes to focus on Him and would call our hearts to respond to Him.

This may sound odd to hear, but make sure this prayer is thoughtful. As much as you are praying for people, you are teaching and leading them at the same time. Really think about what you hope God will do in your community as you gather and then pray for it.

Singing Over the Body

Sometimes the first song in the worship set can be seen as the icebreaker and is often referred to as a "throw away bumper song" while people get settled in their seats. This annoys me because I know that our time in worship is short, and I don't want to be wasteful. One way that I often begin a service is simply by singing the call to worship. You can write something original, put a familiar sounding melody to a Psalm, or even begin with a section from the bridge of your first song in the service. This helps the congregation to quickly focus their attention on the lyrics and your leadership. These moments usually feel quite reverent. If you are creative and intentional, you can keep it from feeling like a performance.

ANNOUNCEMENTS

Once upon a time, in a church far, far away... actually, all the time... in churches everywhere... right after the second song someone awkwardly jumps up on stage, cracks a joke, and has everyone sit down to listen to the current events and activities in each of the church ministries for seven minutes.

Whether the church is expressing a need for volunteers, asking for money and resources, or simply inviting people to join the new church bowling league, the body has now officially become distracted from the story that the first couple of songs were telling. Yikes! At this point I am usually thinking about how I, as the worship pastor, now have to start all over to help the worshippers refocus their attention on God, who He is, and prepare them for the teaching of the Word.

Have you ever driven a car with a manual transmission? Do you remember the learning curve? It takes time and practice to learn how to switch gears in a smooth and seamless way. Yet, so many churches run their services like a 15-year-old learning to drive stick shift! In so many churches, the announcement time is placed in a distracting spot. If we are being honest, most people will probably retain a very small amount of what they experience throughout a 60-75 minute church service. So, it is vitally important to be intentional with where you place announcements.

Find a place in the service that works and connects with the overall flow. Announce the "main things" that pertain to the church as a whole. Be creative and make sure the service host is engaging and to the point. When all else fails, focus on the "majors." Rely on the handout and the pre-service slides and videos to communicate the "minors" and even consider not doing announcements.

TO STAND OR TO SIT

When it comes to certain liturgies, one of the issues that some churchgoers have with it is the amount of standing and sitting that happens. For some people, it is jarring. For others, they may not physically be able to participate in that much sitting then standing. Either way, too much "standing then sitting" is distracting.

To avoid this, you will have to lead well and structure your service flow thoughtfully.

First, it is so helpful to ask your people to either sit or stand. Some of the most awkward moments I have experienced in a corporate gathering have been when half of the people stood or sat at any given time. Take the pressure off the people! You will calm a lot of anxiety with a simple "would you stand with us" or "you all may be seated."

Second, grouping all of your singing together helps with this. If you sing a song and then do announcements, people stood, and then they sat. And now they will have to stand again after for more songs. Then they will have to sit again for the message…. And then stand again for more songs… and, now they are tired and annoyed… or in pain!

Our recommendation is to identify which elements in your service where it is most appropriate to stand and to sit, and then group those together as much as possible. This will keep people engaged.

PRAYER

This is such an important piece of our shepherding leadership from the stage. Praying for and with the people we are leading can be such an impactful moment as we consider what so many of God's people are carrying with them into the gathering. However, we MUST be very careful and aware of our own motives as well as what the Word of God tells us concerning public prayer. In Matthew 6, Jesus Himself gives us some insight and warnings.

"Beware of practicing your righteousness before men to be noticed by them; otherwise you have no reward with your Father who is in heaven" (6:1).

PRAY ABOUT WHAT TO PRAY.   "When you pray, you are not to be like the hypocrites; for they love to stand and pray in the synagogues and on the street corners so that they may be seen by men. Truly I say to you, they have their reward in full. But you, when you pray, go into your inner room, close your door and pray to your Father who is in secret, and your Father who sees what is done in secret will reward you" (6:5,6).

"And when you are praying, do not use meaningless repetition as the Gentiles do, for they suppose that they will be heard for their many words. So do not be like them; for your Father knows what you need before you ask Him" (6:7,8).

All of this is so important for us to keep in mind as we use "small" moments of prayer to connect with the body and to continue the gospel focus throughout the service between songs and in our transitions. As we discussed in the last chapter, the "why," the "what," and the "way" we are praying can quickly become a distraction if we are not thoughtful. Here are a few observations and suggestions from our experience:

WHY PRAY - It creates a more intimate and shepherding connection with the body. It allows for us to agree with one another (AMEN) on who God is, on who we are, and on things going on in our community and our world.

WHAT TO PRAY - Things that pertain to the body as a whole. Things that connect us personally with the lyrics of the songs we are singing. Things that prepare us to open our hearts to the Holy Spirit and the Word of God.

WAY TO PRAY - With humility and sincerity. With confidence and authority. Led by the Spirit and with a heart of gratitude.

WHAT TO AVOID

Repetitive prayers - If we are praying through the same things in the same way every week, it can come across as if our prayers are just a space-filler or a tool for transitions. Rehearsed prayers - These create a sense of fakeness and inauthenticity and become a distraction as the body will quickly pick up on your "prayerful performance." This is also a potential indicator of personal insecurity and self-righteousness.

Long and Lengthy prayers - As a worshipper, these can become the most distracting and frustrating moments in a church service, especially after the congregation wakes up at the end of your prayer. I am sure you know what we are talking about... zzzz!

Overall, it is a good idea to "pray about what to pray."

STRUCTURED FREEDOM

Have services planned out in advance but not set in stone. Relax and let the Spirit lead you and the team through rehearsal. Be willing to add a chorus and even an extra song if the Lord is leading.

Many different service flows and styles of worship are useful and effective. Contextualize your community and figure out what works. Whatever you find that works, do that well.

Just remember that you are the director of the Sunday service. Earlier, Justin mentioned the "movie score." We all know that there is a great difference between watching your favorite movie on DVD and watching your favorite movie on TBS. Watching the movie on DVD allows the viewer to experience the story of the film uninterrupted, whereas the TBS experience includes advertisements every ten minutes.

It is much easier to follow the plot and enjoy a movie when you are able to watch it all the way through. As the director of the service, you can help eliminate these "commercial breaks" by creatively crafting your service to minimize distractions.

Clap your hands, all you nations; shout to God with cries of joy. For the Lord Most High is awesome, the great King over all the earth.
PSALMS 47:1-2

CHAPTER 5

Energy and Emotion

While the service flow is essential to telling the Gospel story every week, the energy with which we tell it is also vital. Our energy and our attitude towards our emotions will have a great affect on our ability to lead well.

ENERGY

If you need noise to fall asleep each night, you would probably choose some form of "white noise." Fans are helpful. Loud air conditioners work as well.

According to the Sleep Foundation, "White noise works by reducing the difference between background sounds and a 'peak' sound."[6] One consistent sound drowns out any other competing sound. White noise prevents you from being disturbed by a change in frequency or dynamic.

A sure-fire way to be "white noise" on a Sunday is to lack energy. We have found that at least three different types of energy affect your leadership each weekend.

One form of energy is sonic energy. While physics plays a role in understanding "sonic energy," for our purposes we are referring to the energy that the music from the stage produces.

SONIC ENERGY

As worship leaders, energy and volume should not be measured equally. Just because a drummer plays with a lot of energy does not mean that the music is automatically loud. However, in a lot of multigenerational churches, there will be a handful of people that automatically conclude that the band is too loud just because they see a drummer pounding away. The physical energy of the drummer can trigger a disconnect with folks that have sensitive ears or are looking for something to complain about.

This does not mean the drummer is doing anything wrong. You may just need to educate and cast vision with certain folks in the congregation to help them understand the facts about volume and energy. We are also NOT saying that your church music is NOT too loud. As you run this topic through the sheep filter, it is worth it to do your research to determine an appropriate volume level for your unique gathering space. Purchase a decibel meter for accountability.

To have an appropriate level of sonic energy in your church no matter what size or music style, you must have a clear and simple vision for your sound and mixing team. Even the slightest EQ and volume issues can completely throw off the sonic energy in the room. This common issue is unfortunately a problem in most churches and can become very distracting. It can also create unwanted conflict between the worship leader and the tech team.

PHYSICAL ENERGY

A second form of energy that comes into play on a Sunday is our own physical energy. The reality is that your congregation will inherit and reflect your energy level. This means that if you are exhausted on Sunday morning and have no energy, the people you are leading will sense that and can become lethargic as well.

ONE OF THE BEST WAYS YOU CAN CONTINUALLY SERVE YOUR PEOPLE IS TO BE HEALTHY EMOTIONALLY, SPIRITUALLY, AND EVEN PHYSICALLY.

On the flip side, if you show up on a Sunday morning refreshed and energized, that alone has the ability to wake up the people you are leading.

If that is true, then we have to make sure that we are taking care of ourselves. One of the best ways you can continually serve your people is to be healthy emotionally, spiritually, and even physically. All of these affect the energy you bring when you gather together.

Having energy on Sunday involves much more than just making sure you get to bed at a decent hour. Physical rest is a byproduct of a healthy rhythm of life. Before you continue reading, it might be a good time to ask yourself:

Does my rhythm and pace of life allow me to rest?

Here are some practical rhythms from our own lives that help us stay rested:

Exercise: I don't hit the gym everyday, but there is always some form of walking, playing (usually disc golf), or working out.

Sleep Schedule: I used to think that as long as I got 7-8 hours of sleep I would be fine. College jacked that up for me. I realized that unless I am going to bed and waking up at around the same time each day, it doesn't really matter how much I sleep! It does not have to be the exact same time, but keeping it consistent helps.

Diet: We could fill another entire book on how to take care of our bodies a.k.a. "the temple of the Lord," but many people have already written books on this topic. You must know that your diet has a greater effect on you than you think. The way you eat and drink can and will become a make or break in your life, marriage, family, and ministry. In essence,

a healthy diet is for both your physical and spiritual health. A poor diet contributes to a lack of energy and motivation. It is also a stewardship issue in our lives and needs to be a very high priority for all of us that bear the name of Jesus. Instead of going over a long list of how to diet well, just take ten seconds and read the nutritional facts and ingredients before you eat something. Also, understand that what you are drinking is typically just as bad, if not worse for your health than the foods you are eating. Certain coffee drinks, energy drinks, beer, and other alcoholic beverages are among a long list of things we drink that aren't good for us . Having self-control regarding what we eat and drink can be a strong indicator of your maturity as a believer and the presence of the Spirit in your life.

From an emotional standpoint, by "healthy," we don't necessarily mean "happy", although that would be great. What we mean is that you have people in your life who can help you process your emotions and unique struggles appropriately. One of the most important things you can ever do is to find a mentor.

Notice we said, "find" a mentor. One thing we strongly believe is that discipleship must be sought out! Don't wait for someone to ask if they can disciple you. Find someone you want to model your life after and ask them. Chances are, if you are wanting to model your life after them, they are probably the type of person who would be willing to pour into your life.

We most likely have all found ourselves smiling on a Sunday

morning while internally we are wrestling with something. That will happen from time to time. But what allows you to lead honestly and appropriately through those times is to have people regularly pouring into your life who know what you are going through.

Having a mentor not only helps your emotional life but also your spiritual life. If you are drained spiritually, it will be challenging to lead week after week. From my own experience, the times when I have neglected to invest in my relationship with the Lord are the times I have felt the pressures of life and ministry the most. Feeling alone in the battle makes you weary.

THIS SPIRITUAL ENERGY IS BEST ACCOMPLISHED WHEN THERE IS AUTHENTIC URGENCY FOR THE GOSPEL IN OUR DAILY LIVES, NOT JUST ON THE PLATFORM.

Being physically tired, emotionally weighed down with no outlet, and spiritually dry all contribute to a lack of energy on Sunday.

SPIRITUAL ENERGY

Finally, the third form of energy that is imperative for a healthy time of worship is the spiritual energy in our church gatherings. This starts with the worship leaders, flows into the band, and then fills the room and the hearts of the people. No, this is NOT a "Sedona, Arizona Spiritual Vortex" kind of energy we are talking about. This is simply the supernatural connection that we experience when we sing

the truth of God's Word together! This spiritual energy is best accomplished when there is authentic urgency for the Gospel in our daily lives, not just on the platform.

Spiritual energy can sometimes develop like a snowball that is formed at the top of a mountain when rehearsal starts. As the band and leaders connect and are unified through the music, their hearts begin to fill up and the energy grows. By the time the service begins, the giant snowball crashes through the roof and suffocates everyone in the room! Just kidding... You know what I mean.

I love reminding myself, my team, and the folks I am leading that our time here is short and the gathering of the saints is such a beautiful gift from God.

EMOTION

There has been a lot of talk about the role that emotions play in our walk with the Lord and in our worship. Some people believe that to truly worship God you must be in touch with all of your emotions. Others believe that emotions can be misleading and therefore should not be trusted as a spiritual compass.

We choose to land somewhere in the middle of that. Emotions can alert us to what is happening on the inside. They can also deceive us about our reality and distort it. But because we are made in the image of God, and God feels emotion, we don't think it is helpful to discard the emotions we feel when we worship.

We also cannot control our emotions at times. When we come together we may be full of joy or full of sadness. And you just can't turn those off.

As a worship leader, the temptation is to measure your "success" of a given weekend by the visible, emotional response of the congregation. The challenge with this is that we will never truly know what God is doing inside of a person at any given moment.

The person in the front who is bowing and crying with hands raised could be having an incredible encounter with the Lord. Or they could be wanting to be seen as spiritual in front of others. The one with their arms at their side whose mouth is barely moving may be completely uninterested by the Gospel. Or, they could be having an incredibly intimate moment of stillness before their King!

You just can't know. But the great news is that you are incapable of producing anything spiritual inside of anyone. And this is great news because that means it is not your responsibility to make anyone "feel" anything. That is 100% the Spirit's job.

If it is the Holy Spirit's job to produce the fruit in the hearts of believers, then our job is to, as we have said before, till the soil. We can do this by making sure that we are singing the truth of

God's Word together in a way that is helpful and understandable.

Emotions can be manipulated and mistaken for a "manifestation of the Spirit." And whatever emotion that is being felt absolutely could be of the Spirit. But again, we never know. So we shouldn't exalt any expression of worship over the other as "more spiritual" because we can never see the heart. We must always allow the Word of God to shape our responses to our emotions.

I cannot tell you how many times leading worship on a big college campus where the same people would break down after every time we worshipped together. And, I can't help but think that it was partly because they were told that if they had a heavy, emotional response to worship then that meant that they were special and spiritual. And, it broke my heart to see these people seemingly experience hurt and brokenness and hoping that our weekly worship gathering could just get them through another week. After a while, if they didn't have this heavy, emotional response to worship, it meant they were not as spiritual as they once were. This is not the truth.

What people need is a life-changing encounter with Jesus and someone to pour into their life, not a really emotional worship set. We can't measure our personal growth in likeness to Jesus by the emotions we feel, so we can't measure the effectiveness of our leadership by emotions that are being felt by others.

Avoid the temptation to measure the "success" of your worship set by how it made people "feel." Instead, measure the effectiveness of your time together by these metrics:

- Was what we sang today true about God and about us?
- Was what we sang today making Christ the center of our attention instead of ourselves?
- Were people engaged and singing together?
- Was your team prepared enough to lead people in worship in a way that was not distracting?

WHAT PEOPLE NEED IS A LIFE-CHANGING ENCOUNTER WITH JESUS AND SOMEONE TO POUR INTO THEIR LIFE, NOT A REALLY EMOTIONAL WORSHIP SET.

When confronted with the Word of God and the truth of the Gospel, there should be some emotional response. When you understand the depth of mercy and grace freely offered to you, it does something to you. But it will always be the Spirit of God doing this in us and other people, and our offering often gets to be the vessel by which it is done.

Emotional responses to worship are NOT a bad thing. There should be this sense of awe, wonder, joy, conviction, and many other emotions as we sing about the God of the universe together! But these emotions just can't be the goal of our corporate worship time.

If you want to just sit in a moment and be still in God's presence, or to sing another chorus, or to speak truth in the middle of your set, do it! God does work through our emotions, and music is an emotive tool. Just don't make an emotional response the "end all, be all" because, as often as our emotions give us helpful insight into our hearts, they are also good liars.

Come, let us sing for joy to the Lord; let us shout aloud to the Rock of our salvation. Let us come before Him with thanksgiving and extol Him with music and song. For the Lord is the great God, the great King above all gods.

PSALMS 95:1-2

CHAPTER 6

Worship Senses

As we have shared before, the role of the worship pastor includes directing and conducting the worship service using a holistic philosophy of worship for the gathering of the saints. We encourage all worship pastors to be thoughtful and intentional with every opportunity they have to point the attention back to the story of God and His purpose. The best way to truly engage the hearts of the saints is through their God-given senses.

WONDER-FULL COMPARISONS

I love comparing a lot of this section to the Disneyland experience. I have learned that Walt's original and simple intentions still hold true to the basic features and vision of Disney's theme parks. Even though several decades have gone by since Disneyland was first opened in Anaheim, California, they have been successful in many ways by keeping the main thing, the main thing… WONDER!

To truly have a high view of God, we must become like little children again with a limitless sense of supernatural wonder! Unfortunately, as we grow up, we also grow in pride, thinking we can figure out God and His ways, limiting our sense of wonder. However, scripture reminds us that His ways are not our ways and His thoughts are not our thoughts (Isaiah 55:8).

In this chapter, we would love to share how our senses can come alive to help engage one another in the wonder and mystery of our God and King during our worship gatherings.

THE BASIC SENSES

It is important to understand that, although our life and relationship to God is often described as "spiritual", we do still experience Him with our usual senses. What we see, hear, smell, touch, and taste all affect the way we experience our world. So what we see, hear, smell, touch, and taste have an impact on the way we perceive God *in the world*. Paul tells us that what can be known about God is something we can clearly see (Romans 1:20).

Now this may seem elementary. And in some ways, it is. We know that we are hearing the music, prayers, and teaching. We know that we are seeing the leaders on stage and the lyrics projected on the screen. But what is worth thinking about is how to create an environment where our senses are best alerted to the "wonder" of who God is.

The purpose of doing this is not to manipulate the senses or emotions, but instead to help everyone who attends the service be completely engaged as we tell the story.

When it comes to a worship environment, no one gave more thought than God Himself. Most of the last 15 chapters of the book of Exodus are devoted to the account of God's dwelling place among the Israelites. There are seemingly endless details about the construction of the ark of the covenant, the tabernacle itself, the courtyard, and the altars. Every detail about the setting of worship was designed to communicate to God's people about His holiness, His purity, and His beauty. The point of this is not to draw a comparison between the tabernacle and our current gathering places but rather to understand how our visual environment can communicate things unsaid and help draw us into a reality bigger than we tend to realize.

EVERY DETAIL ABOUT THE SETTING OF WORSHIP WAS DESIGNED TO COMMUNICATE TO GOD'S PEOPLE ABOUT HIS HOLINESS, HIS PURITY, AND HIS BEAUTY.

THE ARRIVAL

Something happens in my heart and mind the moment I arrive at Disneyland. There's something about that nostalgic sound of the music, the intentional signage, scenery, and visuals that cause me to smile and suddenly become less concerned with the cares and worries of the busy world around me. They have a certain way of engaging our natural and God-given senses to

accomplish their vision in bringing families closer together and setting aside their differences.

>OKAY... TIME OUT... Please don't take my observations about Disneyland the wrong way. Yes, there are many worldly things happening in the not-so-wonderful world of Disney. Some may say that the tactics that they use to attract us and play with our senses is, in essence, a brainwashing tactic. Even though I do think that this might be true in some ways, I strongly believe that there is nothing new under the sun and that there is so much to learn from creative people that were made in God's image even if they are not directing their creations ultimately back to THE Creator. Yes, Disney is a multi-billion dollar enterprise that will do anything, even manipulate human emotions to make a buck. However, we also need to acknowledge the fact that for centuries, even the church and it's leaders are guilty of using and manipulating emotions and senses to push their own evil agendas and false truths for money and unjust gain. I say all this to show the importance of the leaders in the Church to test their own motives and to use discernment and wisdom as we shepherd God's sheep.

So just like when you arrive at Disneyland, it is important that we work hard to engage the senses and begin to prepare the hearts of our church family from the moment they arrive on our campuses. This could be accomplished in many ways through things like the words or the imagery on the signage, the sound of the outdoor music in the background, and the welcoming smiles on the faces of the greeting team. Even the cleanliness around the parking lot and campus can prepare hearts and communicate our vision.

STAGING

We believe that simple and intentional staging is very important for the worship service as it is basically the main visual focal point in the room. First of all, we are not usually encouraging churches to figure out what to add to the stage as much as we are trying to get things removed from it. Every worship space is different as it plays to each church's unique culture and style. Here are just a few quick things to think about when you are literally setting the stage...

THE BACKDROP

Maybe your church likes to change things up often with staging that fits your theme or current series. Even though this might require some extra budget and volunteer coordination, this is a great way to keep things fresh and creative to enhance the visuals. Keep it simple and focused.

THE BAND

It is important for your band to feel connected with each other allowing for easy eye contact and communication with the worship leader and one another. We encourage you to find creative ways to place the band members and vocalists at strategic spots on stage to promote unity with each other which results in unity with the worshippers.

EYE SORES

Did you know that when a drum set is on the stage without a drum shield, people will often draw the conclusion that the music is too loud? It doesn't have to be this way. This is a sad and frustrating reality, especially for drummers as they tend to feel detached from everyone in their little cage. We urge worship teams to develop and train their drummers to "play to the room" so that their volume never becomes an issue. Mature and humble drummers will learn to put the unity of the body before their own musical aspirations.

Less is more when it comes to staging.

LYRICS AND PROJECTION

Have you ever attended a church service where the words on the screen have caused more of a distraction than anything else during the worship time? This is actually a large problem in so many churches. From mis splelligns, grammar, timing and other technical issues, these details have the potential to positively or negatively impact our mission. Let's back up for a quick moment.

Long ago there were these thick books called hymnals. The

hymnal carried the historic and popular songs of the day along with these little black dots with lines called "notes." There were hymnals under every chair or on the back of every church pew for the congregation to reference during the worship time in their services. The senior pastor or music minister would call out the hymn number for everyone to turn to and then he would begin to wave his arms back and forth as the conductor of the congregation. Sounds like a blast right? Keep reading, it gets better!

Have you ever heard of "transparencies?" Transparencies were a thin 8.5 by 11 sheet of plastic with words and images printed on them that you would place on a large projection device at the front of the room. The projection device had a set of mirrors and magnifiers that would project the words from the transparency onto a white screen. This cutting-edge technology would soon take the place of the hymnals in local churches everywhere for lyric references once the contemporary worship songs and style entered into the church.

Now that our advanced modern day projection technology has made our worship gatherings so much easier and practical, there are still some important things to discuss so that we can effectively fulfill our mission in shepherding the sheep. As we have discussed before, there is not and never has been a "one size fits all" worship gathering. However, we believe that there are some helpful tips to keep our gatherings distraction-free and focused on the story of God when it comes to presenting song lyrics and slides.

THE WHO -

Your tech and production team is just as important as your band. So, it is imperative that your production volunteers have a clear understanding of their role in the sound booth just as a drummer or vocalist on the stage. Knowing the value of the part that they play in the service can make all the difference. Because this role of projecting the lyrics is so important, this volunteer needs to be capable of running the technology and following the worship leader and service flow with excellence.

THE TIMING -

If you want to make your production and tech team sweat, go ahead and allow them to keep running the slides two seconds too late. In a matter of moments, worshippers from all around the room will be glaring back at them in frustration. When the lyric slides are even a split-second too late, it can completely deflate the confidence of the worshipper and ultimately kill the energy in the room as they stop singing. I have experienced this so many times. Not to mention how hard it is to lead people in singing as they stare up at you like lost little children...at Disneyland! This needs to be a priority for your team! Remember, the worshippers do not have the songs memorized like you do (I promise, that's the last Disneyland reference).

THE WHAT -

It is crucial to make sure that we are thinking philosophically through the way we are creating these slides. We need to be double and triple checking the grammar and spelling of these songs. Even the slightest error on the screen can quickly pull our attention away from what we're singing. We might also mention the style and size of the font along with how many lines to fit on the screen. We have learned that when you work hard to fit a complete phrase on one slide, worshippers can grasp the message more clearly and it can prevent distraction. For instance, *Oh Lord my God, when I in awesome wonder, consider all the worlds Thy hands have made. I see the stars, I hear the rolling thunder. Thy power throughout the universe displayed.* You should have no problem fitting this entire verse on the screen which will help keep the focus on the overall message that this writer wanted us to understand.

We also understand that the size of each church's building plays a role in how many lines are on the screen. For example, a church that meets in a larger building may not be able to have more than two lines on the screen because the font would be too small for people in the back of the room. At the end of the day, what is most important regarding the projection of lyrics is making sure that whatever you decide to do is what is most helpful for your congregation's participation.

THE BACKGROUNDS -

Wow, this is a touchy one for me personally. The reality is

that many humans do not always need to see a picture of an ocean to help them better identify with the song *Oceans* or an image of a deer next to a creek to grasp the heart behind the old song *As the Deer*. Well, it might actually be helpful to see a live action final battle scene from The Lord of The Rings while singing the last verse of "How Great Thou Art." Ok, you get the point. I am not completely against using backgrounds for songs when it is simple and tasteful. Let's just agree that we don't have to use backgrounds for the sake of using backgrounds to fill the empty space. By the way, I have yet to hear a good reason to use moving backgrounds on a screen during worship. Don't we already live in a world where everything is so busy and constantly moving around us? The best way to lose your train of thought is to throw up some multi-colored swirling lines behind the words that I am supposed to be meditating on. Come on, now. When all else fails, try this...white words, black screen. Let the lyrics tell the story and stoke the imagination and wonder of God.

THE MUSIC, MESSAGE, AND VISUALS SHOULD ALL LOVE AND SUPPORT ONE ANOTHER.

LIGHTING

Another way to engage the senses is to use lighting. All throughout Scripture we read of light and darkness. Light and darkness are both physical and spiritual realities. Part of storytelling is being conscious of the "mood" or emotional moment at any given part of the story.

While it is important to be mindful of how light and darkness relate to storytelling, they play an even more practical role. I have always thought it curious that most churches do not incorporate more natural light. As I have thought about the reason for this, and visited a church building with a lot of natural light, I noticed that it is more difficult for me to become engaged in a story without an engaging setting.

Think of it this way: imagine you went to see a performance of Wicked. Except, instead of seeing it in a magnificent theater in Victoria, England, it took place in your own home. While it may still be entertaining, there is something about the setting in which the story is told that keeps you engaged.

Now, remember, nothing we do can ever enhance the message of the Gospel or give it more power. But what we can do is use every aspect of our services to help people hear it, understand it, and engage it. So we have an opportunity to use lighting to create an environment that promotes more engagement and less distraction.

One year, we had the opportunity to work with a church in transition. Part of the work we accomplished was done in their meeting space. The church was located on a beautiful mountain and had an incredible view. The problem was that the pastor taught right in front of this incredible view. You can imagine the distraction when a pack of javelina wanders through that part of the desert. This is an example of a visual environment that lent itself towards distraction rather than engagement.

In this particular situation, we flipped the room (so the view was at the back), lowered the screens to block the light, and installed a controlled lighting rig. This allowed for the tech team to create an environment that helped keep people's attention on the service and the story.

We would all be surprised as to how little it takes for us to be distracted. Being thoughtful about the visual aspects of our services can help us eliminate many distractions each week.

As a pastor and storyteller, visuals can either be the wind at your back or the wind in your face. They can be the greatest help to your storytelling or the greatest hindrance. The music, message, and visuals should all love and support one another. Part of our job is to use all that we see and hear to communicate the Gospel in a way that promotes engagement and participation.

For since the creation of the world God's invisible qualities—His eternal power and divine nature—have been clearly seen, being understood from what has been made, so that people are without excuse.

ROMANS 1:20

CHAPTER 7

The Songs We Sing

Selecting the songs that we sing every week is one of our most important and frequent tasks as worship pastors.

Worship pastors are teachers. The fact of the matter is that music is one of the most important parts of church gatherings. From my own experience growing up in church, I left the gathering singing a song we sang together more often than I would remember large chunks of the sermon or message. There is a good chance I am not the only one.

This does not mean that our singing together is more important or impactful than the teaching of the Word. It just taps into the fact that as humans we are able to quickly store and remember bits of information when they are presented to us in patterns of sound such as: alliteration, assonance, repetition, and rhyme.

Why is this important?

The words that you choose to sing together on the weekend are embedded in the minds of your people.

Therefore, worship pastors are teachers. So how should we go about choosing songs? First, we have to acknowledge that there is no one way to do this. Most of worship leading begins with being a part of a community that you know, love, and understand. This community allows you to wisely choose songs that will resonate with your congregation.

So it is going to look different for everyone, in every city, and in every environment. But there are a few things that we should be aware of when choosing songs.

Here is a filter we suggest you use when selecting songs for corporate worship: *Is this song true about God and true about ourselves? Are the songs we are singing presenting a clear view of who God is and His character? Is the melody and structure of the song too difficult for people to sing?*

First, lyrically, the songs we sing have to be true about God and about ourselves. It does us no good to use music to emotionally attach the congregation to a wrong idea about God. While we have to make sure that our songs are true, this doesn't mean that all of our songs have to be theologically "deep."

For example, John Mark McMillan's "King of My Heart" echoes a chorus that sings three words. But there's something incredible that happens when groups of people sing a song of trust that rests on the true goodness of God: "You are good." This is an important song for people to sing but it doesn't involve a deep exegesis of a text. People understand it and identify with it easily.

In addition to making sure the songs we are singing are true, I think it is important that the songs we sing are clear. Being an artist is something that is very close to the heart of God. And from the beginning God intended us to be creative (Gen 2). However, sometimes our artistry in worship songwriting can present an unclear and ambiguous view of God and ourselves.

> THE WORDS THAT YOU CHOOSE TO SING TOGETHER ON THE WEEKEND ARE EMBEDDED IN THE MINDS OF YOUR PEOPLE.

What I am saying is that if you listen to a song and think afterwards, "I don't really know what that means," please don't lead this song. Chances are, other people won't really know what it means either and there is probably something better we could sing.

What I am **not** saying is that being really artistic and creative is bad. It's a really good thing, and it is important that talented songwriters continue to write creative songs for the church. And if you don't clearly understand something in a song you hear, that does not mean it is wrong or not helpful. I just don't think it would be helpful in the context of singing with a large group of people, especially when there is not an opportunity to pastorally discuss the possible lack of clarity after.

From a sonic, melodic perspective, the songs we sing should not be impossible to sing. They should be easy to catch on and remember. They should be within the vocal range of the average male or female. This does not mean that we have to sacrifice creativity. Instead, I think it presents an incredible challenge to put our creative efforts towards creating songs and environments that promote singing together.

As we have discussed, worship during our gatherings is telling a story. Worship pastors are in charge of telling the story of the Gospel! In terms of themes, a well-rounded song selection is important. If we only sing songs about how "bad we are," we might quickly forget how good God is. If we only sing songs about Jesus dying on the cross, we might quickly forget that He is alive.

It is important to tell the story of the Gospel, from creation all the way to restoration, as best we can each Sunday to remind our people of the story they are a part of. This is the beauty of singing. It is one of the most unifying human experiences. And no matter where you are leading at or how you lead, we are all part of the same story and we all worship the same King.

KEEPING BALANCE

As Josh shared so well in the last section, there are so many intricate details to consider while selecting songs for musical worship. It is important to line up the "why" with the "how" and "what" when we are planning our gatherings.

Throughout the church in America, and even Europe over the past century, there have been some traditions that have been carried into our modern church culture. Many of these church traditions are timeless and continue to be a blessing to the body and promote unity. However, there are a few traditions that need to be addressed in our church gatherings to better serve God's people in a highly distracted and performance-driven world. For a moment, we would like to discuss the topic of "special songs" or "presented songs" in the service.

PRESENTED VS ENGAGEMENT

With an anti-consumerism mindset, we encourage churches and worship pastors all over the country to run from bad habits that promote a performance and talent-driven church gathering. The best way to break these habits is to identify the traditional performance factors in the service flow. The one we would particularly like to touch on is the "special music" element that, in most cases, tends to point the worshippers to the creation instead of the Creator.

First off, if you only have allotted 25 minutes (5 songs, maybe) of music in your service, wouldn't you like to make sure that this time is well spent to promote the unity of the body by allowing them to sing together? I am NOT saying that it is wrong to have reflective moments in the service flow where we can thoughtfully and intentionally "sing over" God's people with words of encouragement. But I am saying that more often than not, these "presented song" moments can quickly turn into a disconnected yawn fest for the congregation. *This topic usually ticks off the choir and the choir director as they have worked hard for months on this weekly worship performance song.*

On another note, why is it that churches often use a performance song during the passing of the offering? Wouldn't it make more sense to play a vision video or share an announcement or testimony about how the generous giving is actually making a difference in the community? One would naturally think that the body would tend to give more freely when they see firsthand how God is using these resources. Anyway, what I am saying is, don't always assume that the well polished CCM performance song in your service is actually engaging with the body effectively. As we have shared before, our time is "literally" short and it is imperative that we are selecting songs that will keep the main thing the main thing! The church that SINGS together, STAYS together.

THE BIBLICAL PURPOSE OF OUR GATHERING IS TO BE UNIFIED AS ONE AND TO SING AND SPEAK "THE HEART LANGUAGE OF GOD".

HEART LANGUAGE

We could write an entire book on this one topic!
I am sure you have heard the phrase "heart language" in your church community at some point. So what is "heart language"

when used in the worship and music context? Musical heart language is usually described as the nostalgic sound that speaks to or ministers specifically to your own heart. As we have shared before, music has a supernatural way of causing us to remember, recall, and reminisce on where we have been and how we got to where we are now. Our own personal heart language is so important for each of us to identify and grasp as the Lord uses these songs and sounds to bring us back to Himself and to identify with us as His sheep who know His voice. So what does this have to do with how we choose songs for our gatherings?

How do we possibly and effectively capture and value the "heart language" of every person that joins us in our worship gatherings?

The answer? We don't! We don't even try! We have said it before and will say it again and again--the weekend gathering is NOT ABOUT US and our personal heart language. The biblical purpose of our gathering is to be unified as one and to sing and speak THE HEART LANGUAGE OF GOD. It is His heart language that we should all be concerned and excited about when we gather together. God's heart language is our unity and oneness with each other (John 17:20-21).

This topic alone has become possibly one of the most contentious issues in the church today, and it has fueled the worship wars in many churches around the world. This is also the topic that becomes the tipping point for most worship pastors to walk away from church ministry as they have found it impossible to please everyone and to speak everyone's musical heart language. That's because it is impossible! SO STOP IT! We need to stop letting the negative and critical comment cards and emails of everyone's personal worship preference and heart language affect how we lead and plan out our services. This is church consumerism at its worst. As worship leaders, we need to rise above this with intentional shepherding and creative balance as we choose the right songs for this crucial time of singing together! It is possible for us to honor ancient and modern worship traditions and to bridge the generational and cultural divides in our community. We can accomplish this by running our song selection process through the *sheep filter* and having a clear understanding of your church culture and demographics.

Your heart language is so important, valuable, and was given to you by God Himself. This does not mean that the leaders of the church should cater to what speaks specifically to you. We live in a world where we can all access whatever speaks to our hearts on a constant basis. From radio, Spotify, YouTube, and practically any device we can get our hands on. What if we encouraged our church community to engage with their own heart language on their way to church or throughout the week? This would help eliminate the expectation of the weekend church gathering to meet those specific desires. This

would also take a HUGE load off of the church leadership and prevent ministry burnout.

Just as we should not cater to everyone else's needs, we cannot just cater to our own. Part of our task is to strike a balance between what is helpful for our congregation to sing, and songs that move us personally. As with any other part of good leadership, finding this balance requires you to understand the people in your congregation.

While it is helpful to pay attention to what speaks to us, it can't be the only factor in the equation. Just because you personally love a certain worship song doesn't automatically mean that you should teach it! When I first started leading worship as a teenager, I would always sing my favorite songs every set. But what I realized over time was that there were lots of people that were not connecting with all of these songs like I was. Regardless of how much you love a song, run it through the song selection filter. Sometimes the song that is speaking to you in a certain season is the perfect song to sing together! And sometimes it is not. So pay attention to what is ministering to you and run it through the filter!

On the other hand, sometimes the most appropriate and helpful songs to sing are the ones we may not prefer, or may be sick of. Part of being a pastor is leading the way in laying aside your own preference. For example, think of that one worship song that you have led 1,000 times… and rehearsed twice as much as that! It is tempting to put that song in the closet and forget it. But remember, your congregation does not sing it as much as you do! If that song is still true about God and encouraging your community, it may still be worth singing.

This has been a hot topic of conversation in circles I am in. There are a lot of songs that have been released that are "me" focused. These songs contain spiritual content and they are often true about God but the main content of the song revolves around the individual.

While we shouldn't throw out these songs, we should remember that God is the focus of why we are gathering. If we spend most of our 25 minutes of worship together singing about ourselves and all the things we are going to do for God, or about how God makes our lives better, we will be tempted to forget that we exist for Him, not the other way around.

Our encouragement is to keep your worship in terms of song selection heavily Christ-centered. Remember, we sing to give glory to God and encourage one another by remembering the Gospel together!

SONG DISCERNMENT

Should we be scrutinizing the hearts and motives of the writers of these songs?

Should the church community or denomination of the song's origin be a concern?

We have received many questions and comments concerning the "content" and "origin" of certain modern worship songs. There has been a growing urgency among both churchgoers and ministry leaders to consider the worship music that is being born out of certain church establishments, denominations, and worship movements. The enemy has used these concerns to divide and distract the body across the country and around the world. We just wanted to take a quick moment to talk about where we stand as a ministry on this topic.

WE BELIEVE THAT IT SHOULD BE THE HIGHEST PRIORITY OF A WORSHIP PASTOR TO LEAD SONGS THAT ARE BIBLICALLY SOUND AND THEOLOGICALLY TRUE ABOUT WHO GOD IS.

First of all, we believe that it should be the highest priority of a worship pastor to lead songs that are biblically sound and theologically true about who God is. There should be no gray area when it comes to the lyrical content of what we are encouraging God's people to sing as we are held to the highest standard in shepherding God's sheep. This should cause us to be very careful and prayerful about how we choose to bring new songs before the congregation.

So, how do we sift through all of this? Well, everyone must

understand and remember that this is NOT a new issue in the church today. These concerns and discussions have been going on ever since the church began, and not just with song lyrics. It is important for all of us to walk through this with humility, grace, and confidence knowing that you will never please everyone and that if you fervently seek the Lord, He will make known His way to you.

So, should we be scrutinizing the hearts and motives of the writers of these songs? You decide. As far as we know, all of the songs that we have been singing over the years were written by sinful people. What? Oh yeah, it's true! Even our beloved hymns were written by men and women who had some pretty twisted theology and gnarly sinful habits in their lives. Is it possible that even King David wrote a song - a.k.a. "Psalm" - the day after he committed adultery or murder? Sure it is. I can tell you as a songwriter myself that some of my best songs were written in some of my darkest days and in the midst of deep hurt and challenges. This may sound a bit extreme, but we would honestly have to eliminate most of our songs of worship if we truly weighed the hearts and motives of the song writers themselves. This is why I love to give glory ONLY to the Lord and credit to the Holy Spirit when an amazing worship song comes on to the scene and impacts my life and spiritual journey.

Should the church community or denomination of the "song's origin" be a concern? This is a very good question. We will give you a definitive answer once we find a perfect church with the perfect doctrine and the perfect theological foundation. These questions aren't new, however, and I think we can glean some wisdom from a wise pastor that has gone before us.

In September of 1866, after much study and research, Charles Spurgeon put together a collection of psalms and hymns for The Church in London to use for their public, social, and private worship gatherings. In the preface of his song book, he provides somewhat of a disclaimer that addresses so many of the same questions and concerns that we are talking about in this chapter. Here is a small excerpt from the preface:

"Whatever may be thought of our taste we have used it without prejudice; and a good hymn has not been rejected because of the character of its author, or the heresies of the church in whos hymnal it first occurred; so long as the language and the Spirit commended the hymn to our heart we included it, and believe that we have enriched our collection thereby."[7]

We love reminding churches and worship pastors that we are all created in the image of God and that anything we create can be a pure reflection of our Maker. I love seeing how the Holy Spirit can inspire and prompt even the most unworthy candidates to promote the gospel and bring glory to our King. This is one of those mysteries that I think is so cool as a follower: to be used by God despite me. When it comes to the songs we sing, it is truly supernatural to see how the Lord can use a song with a true lyric and moving melody to impact and even transform a life and unite God's people.

How I personally work through this as a worship pastor is quite simple. First, I run the songs through all of our Likewise filters that Josh explained earlier in this chapter. If for some reason I introduce a song that creates confusion or even causes someone to be concerned, I prayerfully consider eliminating it from our song list. No big deal. It is honestly not worth it to me to create a distraction with a song when there are SO MANY others to choose from, even if I personally enjoy it. On the other hand, I am known to take risks at times, and I always encourage worship pastors to try new things and see how the worshippers respond. It is okay to try things and if they don't work... just don't do it again! Remember to keep the balance by remembering WHO you are leading and HOW you are called to shepherd them.

THERE SHOULD BE NO GRAY AREA WHEN IT COMES TO THE LYRICAL CONTENT OF WHAT WE ARE ENCOURAGING GOD'S PEOPLE TO SING AS WE ARE HELD TO THE HIGHEST STANDARD IN SHEPHERDING GOD'S SHEEP.

For accountability reasons, it might be a good idea to run your list of new songs for the year through a panel of wise men and women in your church. The church elders would probably even enjoy having the opportunity to speak into this topic and give their blessing. It is always beneficial to have checks and balances for ministry areas like this. **When someone from the congregation brings their "worship concerns" and comments to you, you will be able to quickly walk them through your simple process and also pass them on to one of the elders if they still have a concern.**

SONGWRITING/REARRANGING

One other balance to keep is the old and new. If you try to introduce too many new songs at once, it may be challenging for the congregation to learn and therefore become discouraging. Too little change and we are tempted to forget that God is doing new things, and we sometimes get sick of the same songs.

One way to keep things fresh is to write new songs! Now, the market for worship music is… crowded… to say the least. But what can be encouraging is to write a new song that is rooted in the past or current experiences of your own community. What is God doing in your church? What is He teaching you? Where do you need to go?

It doesn't have to go on some record! If you can encourage the hearts of the people you love by writing a song that expresses the identity of your people and season as a church, it can go a long way!

Some of the most special times leading worship with Justin were the times when we led a song that we wrote together for our church. There is something extremely unifying about singing something together that is a reflection of your specific season. Because singing together is a great way to remember what God has done and will do, we are encouraged to always be writing new songs!

"Sing to him a new song; play skillfully, and shout for joy."
- Psalm 33:3

"Sing to the Lord a new song; sing to the Lord, all the earth."
- Psalm 96:1

One other way to keep things fresh is to rearrange songs, particularly the old hymns. Writing a new chorus or chord progression to a familiar song can bring lots of life to it! Being able to lead a hymn without it sounding like a hymn (with organ and lots of vibratooooooooooooo!) is a great way to help people, especially the younger people in your church, connect with songs that have a rich history.

HOWEVER! We STRONGLY encourage you to not change the melody or lyrics to the old hymns. The reason for this is because it can easily throw people off, embarrass them, and keep them from singing. There are few things more humiliating in a corporate setting than belting out a song as loud as you can and then singing it wrong. We suggest that the melody and lyrics of the song should remain familiar but you can take liberty to make it fresh in other ways!

CONCLUSION

Song selection is one of the most frequent ways you serve the people in your congregation. Because of this, it is important that we be very thoughtful when it comes to choosing what songs to sing. We encourage you to use the filter given in this section as a starting point for determining what songs are good for your people to sing together.

Sing to Him a new song; play skillfully, and shout for joy. PSALM 33:3

Sing to the Lord a new song; sing to the Lord, all the earth. PSALM 96:1

CHAPTER 8

Volunteers & Team Building

INTRODUCTION

If we look at worship pastoring as a job, the volunteers and team building item on our job description might just be the most challenging to accomplish. When I first officially became a pastor, someone once told me that the best part of my job will be "the people," and the worst part of my job will be "the people." It is very difficult to measure success when it comes to recruiting, instructing, admonishing, and shepherding the staff and volunteers that are serving alongside you. It is difficult because this part of our ministry requires us to have a deeper, vulnerable, and more invested relationship with the people that are serving alongside us on stage or in the tech booth. It is also difficult because many times your team members have personal expectations of you as their leader and pastor that you may or may not be aware of. They may have expectations of you that you will not be able to fulfill. In many ways, as the worship pastor, the people we are serving with can either bring us up or drag us down as we lead God's people in worship. It is the way we shepherd our team and their families that can make all the difference in the church and in our gatherings.

In this chapter we will walk through a number of intentional ideas and suggestions that will put some things in perspective as we lead our worship teams.

THE HEART OF THE VOLUNTEER

There are so many directions that we could take this, but we would like to keep things simple and to the point. Because it is difficult for us to know and discern the condition of the hearts of those we are sharing the platform with, we need to approach this with humility and grace. We also understand the dynamics of recruiting and musicianship are different in each church and that the standards and expectations may vary. Here are just a couple of common questions we want to address as we begin this section:

> IT IS THE WAY WE SHEPHERD OUR TEAM AND THEIR FAMILIES THAT CAN MAKE ALL THE DIFFERENCE IN THE CHURCH AND IN OUR GATHERINGS.

How do we determine who is spiritually fit and qualified to lead with us from the platform?

How do we determine who is musically and technically fit and qualified to be a part of the team?

How do we empower our musicians to grow in their spiritual, musical, and technical gifts and abilities?

FIRST THINGS FIRST

We are strong believers in and advocates of putting quality of heart on stage before quality of skill and talent. Much of the time you can have both, but not always. When some churches put musical excellence before spiritual integrity, they find themselves on shaky ground. We'll explore why in this chapter.

However, we have found that inviting someone who is not a believer to serve with us on Sunday has provided an incredible opportunity to share the Gospel.

This is why we encourage worship pastors to be discipleship-driven! If our goal as worship pastors is to develop a team that is unified and on mission together, it requires us to be more invested in the lives of these team members both spiritually and musically. Here are a couple of quick stories for some perspective...

There was the time when a non-believing bass player in the community was invited to play bass on a Sunday morning for the worship service. This bass player loved to play in bands and was intrigued by the opportunity so he showed up. The worship pastor was able to use the stage as an opportunity to develop a deeper relationship with this bass player which ultimately led to a complete transformation of this man's life as he committed himself to following and serving Jesus. Within a few months, his entire family was attending this church and were completely devoted to the Lord. Today this man is the discipleship pastor on staff at a church in Arizona!

There was another time when one of our musicians showed up for Sunday morning rehearsal smelling like booze and completely hung over. He was quickly pulled aside and sent home. After a couple months of intentional care and shepherding, he was restored to serving on the worship team and filled with an extraordinary amount of grace and peace. He was able to see that we loved him more as a brother than we did as a crucial part of the band.

There was also that time when after a few months of joining the worship team, this keyboard player with "great chops" decided that he would put his own musical preferences before all others and show off his skills during the service. After almost derailing the worship train and forcing me as the worship pastor to have him muted in the house, he was asked to step down for a short season to consider his actions and to deal with the ego and pride. After a month of trying our best to walk alongside him, he ended up leaving the team and bashing mine and the church's name throughout the community... And we lived happily ever after!

And finally, there was this amazing local rock musician in our community that had been in and out of the church his whole life. He was very well known as a native in our town and was often performing the awesome 80s rock hits in the bars and on the community events stages, usually sponsored by Jack Daniels. When his life began to take a rough turn as a husband and family-man, he found himself being impacted by the Word of God and the worship ministry at the church I was serving at. The worship pastor at the time saw an opportunity to make a big gospel impact not only in this man's life, but for the whole community. This worship pastor made the "go and make disciples" mission look easy. The local rock star watched the power of Jesus transform his life, his marriage, and his family before his eyes. He eventually walked away from the world of performance that he so loved and committed his life and musical gifts to the mission of uniting God's people in worship. He is now one of the most passionate and humble worship pastors that I know. And to say his entire community has been impacted by the light that he shines would be quite an understatement!

I could go on for pages telling you so many stories, both amazing and frustrating, about working with the volunteer members of the worship team. I'd love to share with you a few pointers that I have learned along the way.

WIDEN YOUR GUARDRAILS

I encourage worship pastors to be thoughtful about the width of our guardrails and expectations for inviting people to join the "volunteer" team. As you read in the stories above, it is very possible and healthy to have an evangelistic approach with your musicians and tech team. Though, I usually draw the line in most cases with the microphone. If we are going to allow new or non-believers on stage, we need to be careful about what is being said through the microphone. I have learned that it is best to let your vocalists know it is better that they just sing and leave the talking to me. Better yet, even for the worship leader, less talking is best.

Be sure to have a clear understanding of what your recruiting guardrails really are. If it is not clear, then you will have to do a lot of cleaning up later with folks that either are included or excluded from the team for various reasons. In other words, there needs to be consistency in the way you recruit and implement team members.

LEGALISM

Legalism is a killer of community and relationships. There was one season as the worship pastor at a church where I was expected to enforce a very legalistic set of rules and expectations on the worship team members that the senior pastor created. We were all actually required to sign a "code of conduct" contract before stepping on stage. It was probably the most difficult and hurtful season as a pastor that I can remember and was the catalyst of my intense struggle with ministry burnout and depression. I had to watch almost half of my worship team members either leave the church or completely resent me and the overall church leadership. Even though I am not against having a simple "desired list of expectations" for our volunteers, I love to encourage worship pastors to keep a healthy and biblical balance of truth and grace as we set these guardrails and protocols for our team members.

LEGALISM IS A KILLER OF COMMUNITY AND RELATIONSHIPS.

PAY TO PLAY - Worship Gigging!

In this book, we have talked a lot about consumerism in the American church and we believe that it is the strongest contributor to the burnout of thousands of worship pastors around the world. So much of this consumerism is rooted in a toxic and unbiblical desire by modern church leaders to be attractional instead of discipleship-driven with our ministry goals. Unfortunately, many worship pastors have fallen into the trap of contributing to this mission and have built their worship philosophy and vision around this performance-driven culture. In many cases, this has disrupted what once was a beautiful and unifying piece of our weekly gatherings. Earlier in the book, we talked about the importance of churchgoers bringing a "sacrifice of praise" into the house of the Lord. We believe this biblical mandate should be clearly understood by the church leaders first before we can expect our church family to fully grasp this command. This is a great "lead by example" opportunity for all of us as we open up the doors for people in the church to use their gifts to serve the Body. We are strong believers in the fact that everyone, yes everyone, has something to contribute and sacrifice for the Church and that all of our various gifts are beautifully equal and useful in the eyes of the Lord (Romans 12:4-8). Unfortunately, there is a certain practice in many churches these days that has greatly impacted our unity, joy of serving, and overall spiritual growth. This brings us to the "Pay To Play" discussion, also known as "Gigging."

Before we get into this, you must know that we strongly believe that those who are called as pastors, directors, support staff, and any other church "staff" position should be financially compensated and cared for as they serve the Body. We also believe that these gifted individuals should be "paid in full" and not "paid in fair." Meaning, in most cases we have learned that church and ministry leaders are often underpaid and given a "fair market" salary instead of what is right and fitting for their work load. But with worship "volunteers", this should be seen differently.

I don't know about you, but it is curious to me that a nursery worker can arrive on Sunday morning at 6:00am to get everything ready for children's church with a smile on her face, ready to love these kids, and never once has it come to her mind that she should be paid for the sacrifice of her Sunday morning. In many churches, she shows up 50 Sundays a year eager and ready to serve! All the while, in the worship center (you know where I'm going with this) the drummer and bass player are on the clock as worship contractors getting paid for their time. This creates a church where the paid musicians are seen by the body and even see themselves as a more important and more valuable part of our church gatherings.

Now, please don't take this EXTREME comparison the wrong way. We do not want anyone to see this as a hand slap to the churches that are participating in this pay-to-play model. We are just hoping that this will cause us all to think deeper about our motives as we build our teams, make disciples, and lead our people with a heart of service and worship. In a way, when we embrace this pay-to-play concept in our churches, we are essentially stealing the opportunity for our musicians to contribute their gifts like everyone else. We have, in essence, become enablers of entitlement.

Do you see now what this concept may be doing to the heart of the musician and servant of Christ? Esteeming their gifts above others, not to mention what it is doing to their ego? Why should the gift of art be valued more than the gift of hospitality or serving kids? In many cases, it is possible that our current church culture is raising up a generation that has no idea what it means to serve or sacrifice in the Body of Christ. This ministry model is killing our culture and pulling us away from the joy of serving. There is really only one way to overcome this kind of thinking and behavior in the Church. We need to run from this performance-driven church model and come back to the heart of worship. When performance, entertainment, and attraction is NOT the priority, you will see a greater sense of unity and faithfulness in your people. FYI, if you choose to make the change back to volunteers, you will probably lose some musicians and even see a dropoff in musical quality. However, we can guarantee that it will grow the overall morale and combat the entitlement culture in our churches!

All in all, we desire to encourage pastors to disciple, equip, and remind those who serve alongside them in worship that there is great reward and joy found in sacrifice and in serving the church.

SOME ANSWERS TO SOME GOOD QUESTIONS ABOUT THIS TOPIC:

• But what if we can't find a drummer for this coming Sunday service?

Do a simple acoustic set! Is it really that simple? Yes. Here is why: there are people all over the world that only wish they had drums even once in their church's lifetime. There are those around the world who worship the Lord in buildings with dirt floors and leaky roofs. The point is that at the end of the day, having a drummer is a luxury, not a necessity. God can be worshipped in spirit and truth and honored no matter what the instrumentation is. So take that pressure off of yourself. Obviously, having a full band is helpful for many reasons. But the moment that we require anything to worship God, that thing becomes an idol.

WE DESIRE TO ENCOURAGE PASTORS TO DISCIPLE, EQUIP, AND REMIND THOSE WHO SERVE ALONGSIDE THEM IN WORSHIP THAT THERE IS GREAT REWARD AND JOY FOUND IN SACRIFICE AND IN SERVING THE CHURCH.

• *How do I respond to my boss who expects me to have a full band every Sunday?*

With grace and patience.

As the worship pastor, we tend to think about worship in these ways more than our bosses do. Sometimes, as churches, it is easy to play the comparison game and not even realize we are doing it. I have heard many different reasons as to why there needs to be a full band every weekend. Almost always, these reasons find their roots in some sort of fear. Typically, the fear is about people liking the music, which is really a fear about whether or not a certain person or group of people will stay at our church or go to the church down the street.

We have to realize that as worship pastors, we don't share the same responsibilities and pressures that senior pastors do. We often do not even share the same perspective. But, that is precisely why we have an opportunity to be a good "teammate." When fear settles in for the senior pastor (in the form of needing a certain style or instrumentation for it to be worshipful), we have the opportunity to calm the storm. And we can do this by having a "why" for why we don't need drums (see above answer) and asking our senior pastor to trust us.

THE MOMENT THAT WE REQUIRE ANYTHING TO WORSHIP GOD, THAT THING BECOMES AN IDOL.

At my church, I went out on a limb and led by myself with just an acoustic guitar. I had done it plenty of times before, but there was fear that it was going to be too different for our people and lack energy. The response that I got from that weekend was incredible. It was "refreshing" for a change. "We could hear everyone singing together!" Those were the types of responses. Because I was able to demonstrate the truth I believed in, trust was established.

So, practically, have conversations with your pastor. At the end of the day, you must submit (in a willful, loving way) to your pastor as best as you are able. It is incredible the weight that can be lifted off of the senior pastor's shoulders by having a worship leader with a biblical philosophy and understanding of worship.

• *How do we transition from a paid musician team back to a serving worship team?*

Earlier in the book we talked about having a "why" for your "what." This comes into play again here. At the end of the day, you cannot control who stays on your volunteer team. So if you believe that making the transition is the right call for your community, make sure to communicate that clearly to everyone at the same time.

We suggest that you don't stop "cold turkey" in making this transition. For starters, if your whole team decides to leave, you will start recruiting from square one and be all by yourself! Giving this transition time allows you to have further conversations with your team, continue building relationships, and prepare for the future.

• Could this ministry model promote sinful motives and behaviors?

Yes. Whenever you decide to pay someone to play at your church, there is always some underlying motivation for that decision. Why do we have to make sure we have a professional guitarist or drummer? Why can't we roll with what we have? These questions must be asked. And the answers to these questions can potentially illuminate certain motivations for the Sunday gathering.

• Is being excellent musically and having good production bad?

No way. I believe it should be our goal to be as excellent as we can possibly be to give God glory and to help our people participate. As we have talked about, good and tasteful lighting can be instrumental to that as well as a tight band. The point is that we never want to be excellent for excellence's sake or to get more people to come to our church instead of the church down the street. The motivation for our excellence should be the glory of God and service to our congregation.

Each church must understand what the aim of their ministry is. Is it to care for people or is it to build a bigger ministry? Is it to love and serve the present community or compete with the church down the street? While the "pay-to-play" model doesn't automatically mean a church has "wrong" motives, before a church decides to model their volunteer team that way, we encourage them to consider the underlying motivations for such a decision.

RECRUITING TIPS

Recruiting for some people is really natural. For some, it can be challenging. Some people just have that personality, the "woo" as Strengthsfinder would call it. Others of us do not!

Justin is the type of person who sees you playing the cello on the sidewalk and invites you to play with him on Sunday. I am the type of person who would really prefer it if you came up and asked me to volunteer!

No matter your personality type, recruiting is essential to your task as a worship pastor, and it often takes work. And sometimes, that work is challenging. So here are some tips and stories from an introverted "not-so-natural" about recruiting your team!

If you want to recruit and develop a volunteer team, you have to **keep your eyes and ears open**. Every once in a while you will get someone who comes up to you and tells you that they have been playing in church bands their whole lives and want to serve on your team. That is amazing. But the number of those people, I would wager, is smaller than the number of gifted people in your congregation that have never been involved!

In order to empower people to serve, you have to get to know them. It's not everyday that God drops a cello player on your sidewalk. There are a lot of gifted people in your congregation who have gifts to give that either don't know how to be involved or have not been invited to participate. You will never know unless you engage them. This takes relational effort on your part. Most people won't initiate a relationship with you because you are on stage. But it can be a real blessing to people when you initiate conversations and relationships. You should do that with everyone anyway, but every once in a while you will discover that this middle-aged man used to play in a funk band and is an incredible bass player.

One of the biggest barriers to people wanting to join the worship team is often that it feels exclusive to them. The more you can engage with your entire church before or after service (your team too!), the more people will feel like your team is not some clique they can never join.

I have been in situations where someone in the congregation has come up to me and told me about someone else who is really gifted. If this happens to you, make sure to follow up! While you can do your best to engage people, you can't engage everyone. So take these "leads" as a gift. If you are having trouble identifying potential volunteers, do not be afraid to ask people in your congregation if they know anyone who may be interested.

One of the best things you can do is to empower your worship team to help you in this area. Chances are, your volunteers know other musicians! Your own team can be a great foot in the door for some people who are unsure of whether or not they want to serve.

Another barrier to recruiting volunteers is our own expectation. While we need to make sure that we are striving for excellence, we may need to "widen the guardrails" as Justin put it when it comes to the skill level of those we are recruiting. You must be the judge of whether or not you can get through a set, but it can be so rewarding to allow people room to grow as a musician under your leadership.

The reality is that there are potentially some significant headwinds for anyone who begins to recruit volunteers. For starters, lots of churches pay their musicians! That is automatically a draw for some musicians. Second, if you are just starting at a church, most of the musicians you know are already plugged in somewhere else.

It can be easy to get discouraged and think that you have failed in the area of recruiting musicians. What you may need to hear is that success does not equal a full band every Sunday. That can be very helpful. But you can do your job effectively regardless of instrumentation. Do the absolute best with what you have and continue to engage people in relationships.

For the most part, recruiting volunteers is a relational endeavor. But no matter what you try, the **single most important** thing you can do is **pray**!

While this sounds so elementary, it is powerful.

When I started a position as a worship pastor at a small church, I was in the exact position I just mentioned. We could not afford to pay musicians, and all of my talented friends were already plugged in elsewhere. The one drummer that was at the church left shortly after I got there to take a staff position at another church.

In the midst of the pressure I was feeling, I started to get discouraged after a couple months. After exhausting every option so it seemed, I just prayed. I asked that God would provide what we needed.

That next weekend I had two guys I had never met before come up and introduce themselves to me and let me know they both play drums and want to serve.

Now, I am not promising that it will happen to you in the same way. But I want to remind you that God knows your need and ultimately is the provider for you and your team!

One last note about that story… One of the drummers who originally told me he wanted to serve texted me later and changed his mind. He said he was too busy. This was definitely a bummer for me. But I had the opportunity to keep engaging him in a small group that we were in.

During this period of a few months, we developed a friendship that existed with no expectation of his service. One weekend, I had a drummer back out on Friday (The bane of our existences… am I right?). So I decided to reach out to my new friend.

Because he was my friend, he obliged to help out that one weekend. The service went great and afterwards he told me this: "Man, that was actually really great. I think I needed that. Let me know whenever you need anyone. I would love to play more."

I would have been friends with this guy regardless of whether or not he ever served. But, because of our friendship, he took a step to help me out and found that he really did want to be a part of it. Relationships are so important!

VISION/CULTURE DEVELOPMENT

One of the most important things you can do as a leader of a team is to clearly communicate your vision. Some people may think that the "worship team" is pretty self-explanatory. Some may simplify it to mean that the vision for the worship team is to lead worship. But hopefully by now in this book, you know that there is much that goes into shepherding the flock that we don't consider.

During a difficult season of ministry for me, I had many of my convictions about corporate worship challenged. While this took its toll on me in different ways, the result of this conflict ended up being really impactful. I was forced to figure out why I believed the certain things that I did and why I believed in a certain philosophy of worship. This journey is one I hope we all go on at some point.

WHEN YOU KNOW WHY YOU ARE LEADING THE WAY YOU ARE, YOU WILL BE ABLE TO LOVE THOSE WHO DISAGREE WITH YOU AND TO STAND FIRM WHEN OPPOSITION TO YOUR LEADERSHIP COMES.

At the end of this season of ministry, I emerged with not only convictions, but with reasons for them. I finally had a "why" behind my "what." This is a place we should all come to not just about worship leadership but about every part of our lives.

The reason having a "why" is so important is because it is really at the heart of leadership. Any leader can give commands, and when they're followed, the job gets done. However, being able to effectively communicate the reasons behind your expectations for your team yields trust, commitment, and passion.

I took my first job as a worship pastor when I was twenty years old. I inherited a tight-knit volunteer team who really loved the worship leader that was there before me. Leading in that environment was really difficult.

About four months in, I finally called a meeting with the whole team. In this meeting, I spent five minutes laying out my expectations for the team and the rest of the meeting explaining why. I had two volunteers come up to me after the meeting to let me know that they no longer wanted to serve. The rest of them, however, were night and day from then on out in terms of their preparation and commitment.

Not everyone will agree with what you want to accomplish and how you want to get it done. This can be absolutely deflating if you don't know why you have certain convictions. But, when you know why you are leading the way you are, you will be able to love those who disagree with you and to stand firm when opposition to your leadership comes. And unfortunately, it will!

So take the time to seek the Lord and understand the "why" behind your "what". Then, effectively communicate this to your teams in love and with confidence.

PREPARATION

The quickest way to burn out your volunteers is by NOT communicating vision, direction, and expectations to them.

We have learned that all worship pastors have different ways of leading, preparing, and communicating in each of their contexts. If everyone on your team understands you, your personality, and your leadership style up front, it's going to make things a lot easier down the road and will help prevent unnecessary conflict and frustration. Without going too deep into details on this matter, we simply encourage all of our leaders to be open and vulnerable with volunteers from the beginning. When we are honest about certain things such as worship team standards, expectations, musical and creative freedom, and personal character, it truly opens a door for deeper relationships with your team. This also creates an environment of peace and safety for your volunteers to feel like they are part of something greater than just a music gig.

TEAM BUILDING & APPRECIATION

How you show your appreciation to your worship team can make all the difference when it comes to the morale and culture in your church. It also can greatly impact the longevity of those who are giving of their time to serve alongside you. We encourage worship pastors to be very intentional when it comes to saying thank you and making your team and their families feel valued. It is more than worth it to even create a budget item for team building and appreciation. Here are a couple basic tips that have worked for me and have made a lasting impact on my volunteers over the years.

- A hand written card a couple times per year can go a long way
- A birthday phone call or text
- Lunch or coffee with each team member a couple times per

year or even a double date with your volunteer and his/her spouse.

- An annual appreciation event or dinner for the whole team When I was a worship pastor in Phoenix, we would put on a fun dinner theater event each year in the form of a game show for our volunteers and their spouses. It allowed us to eat and laugh together and to build a stronger sense of community with each other.

CARE & CONCLUSION

Finally, it is critical that we understand the health of our volunteer team is a reflection of our leadership and the overall vision of the church. This is why we highly encourage pastors to have a heightened awareness and availability for the personal needs of those they are serving with. Whether a team member is physically sick, spiritually struggling, working through challenges in the home and marriage, or even just feeling distant, it is imperative that we keep an eye on these things. When we make ourselves available and show that we are aware and concerned about them, it truly makes a volunteer feel at peace and connected to the body. Be sure, however, not to overload yourself with all the burdens of your team as you can exhaust and even burden yourself and your own family. Keep things in balance and let your love for your team be worked out more in action than in words.

For just as each of us has one body with many members, and these members do not all have the same function, so in Christ we, though many, form one body, and each member belongs to all the others. We have different gifts, according to the grace given to each of us. If your gift is prophesying, then prophesy in accordance with your faith; if it is serving, then serve; if it is teaching, then teach; if it is to encourage, then give encouragement; if it is giving, then give generously; if it is to lead, do it diligently; if it is to show mercy, do it cheerfully. ROMANS 12:4-8

CHAPTER 9

Relationships

Up to this point, we have talked a lot about the importance of building relationships. In addition to your relationship with your volunteers, we have the opportunity to build healthy relationships with our staff and people in our congregation. Building these types of relationships is different than building relationships with your volunteers because they both present unique, unavoidable obstacles.

When it comes to the relationship you have with other staff members, you enjoy a unique set of responsibilities with a unique flexibility that many other people on your staff do not have. This is a potential barrier to a healthy relationship. Not only that, but you also are on the platform! Everyone knows who you are and sometimes that is also a barrier to your relationship with other staff members.

With those in the congregation, the fact that you are on the platform is a barrier in and of itself. Some people won't approach you because of your position while many others believe deep down that you don't want to have a conversation with them.

In all of these, it is our responsibility, as followers of Jesus, to lead and love from a posture of humility. Because of the nature of your role, it may fall on you to tear down these potential barriers. While it can be hard work, it will always be worth it.

Being a part of a church staff is the same as being on a team. Because this is true, there are certain realities of our roles that we need to accept and attitudes we need to avoid to be a good "teammate."

IMPORTANT REALITIES ABOUT YOUR JOB

As worship pastors, it is critical that we understand the importance of our highly influential role in the local church as we feed, tend, and take care of the sheep. We must acknowledge some hard, yet important realities about our role. We like to use our "75/25" perspective to better understand this. In most cases, 75 percent of our job on staff at a church is going to fulfill our passions and allow us to use our natural and God given gifts. However, 25 percent of our job requires us to do things that are just plain frustrating, challenging, and at times unfulfilling. This 25 percent may be

IT IS OUR RESPONSIBILITY, AS FOLLOWERS OF JESUS, TO LEAD AND LOVE FROM A POSTURE OF HUMILITY.

the Lord's reminder to you that you are not in heaven yet and that you still have a lot to learn as a leader. We encourage you to be aware of the fact that not everything you do on staff at the church is supposed to bring you complete joy.

Artistic people can tend to elevate and even segregate themselves in the church world as a misunderstood and undervalued group of leaders. Even though we can understand and even sympathize with this notion, we want to urge all worship pastors to be humble as you work alongside the rest of the church leadership. No, you do not have all the answers and no, your creative way of doing things is not the only way. We want to invite you to consider breaking through some of the stereotypes that artists, in the form of worship pastors, have been pulled into.

BREAKING THROUGH THE "ARTIST" STEREOTYPES

- **"Artist Standard Time":** it has been suggested that musicians operate on their own time schedule. Out of respect for the people on our staff that have their own roles and responsibilities, we have to make sure to be punctual. Being late for meetings communicates to others that we believe we have our own set of rules. Honor the others on your staff by being on time.

- **"Artists Are Not Administrative":** it is often assumed that creatives and artists are hard to get a hold of and that they have trouble communicating. As pastors, we have to make sure that we are as available as we can be for communication with our volunteers and our staff. This means we have to be replying to emails, phone calls, and text messages relatively quickly. This communicates that we care about those in need of our communication and that we are available to them.

- **"Artists Have Tunnel Vision":** It is not uncommon for worship pastors to be accused of not connecting with other ministries outside of worship. We must make it a point to not only engage with our other staff members relationally, but to be engaged with their ministries and available to serve them.

- **"The Artist's Work on a Pedestal":** it is common for some artists to believe that their art is more special, helpful, or beneficial to the Body than other types of work. This encouragement from a mentor of ours is worth mentioning: artists must put their art on the altar rather than the pedestal. Artists in the Kingdom are to be servants.

THE SENIOR PASTOR

Unfortunately, because of the way we usually "do church" in America, the relationship between the senior pastor and the worship pastor can become one of the most contentious relationships on staff. The reason for this comes down to 2 words: POWER and GLORY!

Isn't it crazy that a senior pastor can spend seven years or more in college and seminary in order to be hired at a church

as the lead pastor while at the same time, a gifted musician and worship leader can be hired as the second most visible and influential pastor on staff with only a basic ministry education or without even finishing high school? Woah! Whether you think this is fair or not doesn't matter. It is a reality, and according to Scripture, there is nothing wrong with this picture (1 Tim 4:12). The only bummer about this is that we live in a selfish and fallen world where we tend to value credentials over calling. I share this not to create division or to puff up the worship pastor, but to create awareness of how our worldly standards have worked their way into the church.

The truth of the matter is, many senior pastors have come to realize that they cannot fulfill the vision of their church and accomplish their goals without a worship pastor by their side. They have learned that today's churchgoers will likely decide where to attend church by the music and overall experience of the gathering before even listening to a sermon. Even though we at Likewise disagree with this way of choosing which church to attend, it is the reality of the world we live in.

Unfortunately, these dynamics can create tension between the senior pastor and worship pastor if they do not work hard to stay on the same page and be unified while they serve together. This is why we encourage worship pastors to communicate well, be quick to forgive, submit to authority, and show grace and love towards their senior pastor and bosses. It is also crucial for worship pastors to exercise humility and maturity when conflict comes along. Also, be aware of the schemes of the enemy and how he would just love to use the hunger for power to cause senior pastors and worship pastors to be at odds with each other. The enemy also delights in creating a rift between the senior pastors and worship pastors when perhaps the time of worship was a "home run" in people's eyes and the sermon was just a "base hit" or vice versa.

OTHER STAFF

The role of the worship pastor can also cause conflict and in some cases, a game of comparison with other pastoral and church staff members as they observe your role and level of influence on the team and from the stage.

Due to the nature of our job description and as the conductor of the weekend gathering, we have to make a lot of decisions about what happens on Sunday. There are times where we may find ourselves stuck while trying to balance the requests and desires of the senior pastor and all the other staff members who are needing stage time and church-wide communication. This can cause problems as worship pastors can be people pleasers and will tend to sacrifice worship vision to appease the staff and to avoid conflict.

It is important that we exercise humility in these cases. Being a good team player allows you to do your part to keep the unity on the team. But we also challenge you to not allow politics and agendas to sneak in to the process.

All of these little challenges are helpful in thickening up the skin of church leaders so that we can lead with confidence and without insecurity.

TECH TEAM

I think I speak for most worship pastors when I say that probably the most difficult place to be standing on a Sunday morning is behind the soundboard. This location in most churches has a vortex, a magnetic black hole for negativity and complaints. It has been said before that "anything and everything that goes wrong in the church is the sound guy's fault!" Even though this is kind of funny and can be fun to joke about, we need to all be aware and reminded of how important and valuable the tech team is, especially the sound guy or tech director. This is why it needs to be a top priority for a worship pastor to be on the same page with the tech director no matter what it takes. It is of the highest importance that the tech director knows that you have his or her back at all times.

Speaking from my own experience, after stumbling along the way, I was able to develop a deep and meaningful friendship with my tech director at my last church, and this healthy relationship made for an amazing seven years of serving together. I also must say that this healthy working relationship really made all of our weekly rehearsals and worship services run smoother.

It is also easy for the worship pastor and tech director to be at odds with each other and to experience unwanted conflict, mainly due to a difference of musical style and opinion. Over the years, I have experienced quite a few difficult tech guys that let their egos and the power from the soundboard get to them. There was even this one time when the sound guy exercised that power by using the forbidden red mute button to prove a point. Even though it is normal for most creatives to naturally struggle with technologically-minded people, it's worth the hard work to stay on the same page together and keep the main thing the main thing: Unity!

No matter what, it is important that we work hard to appreciate all of the volunteers and staff who are serving behind the scenes to help make things happen and create a beautiful service.

PASTORAL CARE

Our personal connection and relationship with the church Body can actually be the thing that wakes you up every morning with an eagerness to get to work. This is naturally because of how we are made by God to love Him and to love others as He loves us. The love we have for the sheep truly allows us to lock in with the heart of God and fulfill our ultimate calling as a pastor.

This love and passion came alive in my heart when I started being more intentional and detailed in my shepherding role, specifically through pastoral care.

When I was just beginning in my role as a worship pastor, the Lord opened my 26-year-old eyes to something that changed me forever. There was this man that would sit in the back of the room every Sunday with his wife. He was a tall and stern old fellow, and he would make it a point to go out of his way every Sunday morning to say to me, "Tuck in that shirt young man." After the first few terrifying encounters

WE ENCOURAGE YOU TO BE AWARE OF THE FACT THAT NOT EVERYTHING YOU DO ON STAFF AT THE CHURCH IS SUPPOSED TO BRING YOU COMPLETE JOY.

with this guy, I found myself avoiding him on a weekly basis. This was partly because he scared the snot out of me and also because there was no chance I was going to tuck in my shirt! Well, after a few months in my role as the worship pastor at this church, I was assigned to my first solo "Pastor On Call" hospital visit. I had done only one of these before as a shadow to our senior pastor, but had no idea how intimidating and nerve racking a hospital visit would be on my own. Anyway, I was informed that a woman in her early 80s was approaching her last moments of life on earth after having a stroke, and it was time for me to step into her hospital room. I had already burned about 480 calories in the elevator on the way up to the 5th floor from my rapid heart rate, but all of my anxiety and fears came to a screaming halt when I pulled back the curtain to see a man kneeling next to her, completely broken. It was him...the "tuck in your shirt" guy that I had been avoiding for weeks! It was at that very moment where I knew that the Holy Spirit was about to do some much needed work on my heart. After about 20 minutes of just sitting and listening to this man share some stories about his wife's failing health and condition, I asked him if I could pray for him and for his wife. He said yes and after praying, we both stood up, he shook my hand and said, "Thank you, pastor." I gave him my card and told him to call me if he needed anything. His sweet wife went home to be with the Lord the next morning.

Five mornings later, I was about to step onto the stage to begin our 8:00am Sunday service when I felt a tap on my shoulder. I turned around and this tall old man gave me the warmest hug and then with a choked-up voice said, "It means so much to me that you would come and sit with me at the hospital. After you left, I felt an amazing sense of peace, and I just wanted to say thank you again." I said, "You are very welcome, and it blessed me so much too." Then he smiled and said, "Now, tuck in that shirt."

Up until that point in my life, I don't think I have ever smiled that much from the stage. Just the fact that 20 minutes on a Tuesday afternoon at the hospital could make such a difference in someone's life made me feel so happy. And, then I started thinking about how much I enjoyed the feeling of doing kind things and caring for people in this way. It was at this point that I began to really understand what it means to be a pastor.

A few years later this man passed away, but there was not a Sunday that went by where he didn't go out of his way to give me a warm hug and tell me, "Good morning." It's funny because he totally got over the untucked shirt thing as he was able to see what was in my heart.

THIS MAKES ALL THE DIFFERENCE

Pastoral care is one of the most obvious and natural roles as we serve in the local church. No matter what your personality type is, we are all commanded by God to love one another and to make disciples in this way. We strongly believe that in the church, however, this role is not just assigned to one pastor on staff. We should rest easy knowing that we are able to share this heavy load with the others and that it should not consume the majority of our time. It is also good to remember that even the most simple gestures of kindness can make all the difference in the lives of the people that we are serving.

No matter how you see yourself as a leader in the church, there is no way to escape the fact that the people you are leading are looking up to you. Whether they express it or not, they see you as an authority and a shepherding figure in their lives. The stage has a unique way of shining a figurative spotlight on the individuals who stand on and lead from it. So you can imagine the impact when the pastors from the stage connect face to face and one-on-one with the people in the seats. This is why it is important for you to remember there are some basic connecting points that allow your care as a pastor to shine into their lives.

Stop sitting in the green room before, after, and in-between services. You can relax at home later. Mingle your way throughout the congregation and let the folks you are leading know that you "see" them and care for them. Greet them by name. Ask specific questions about what you already understand about them: health, family, struggles, and prayer requests. Make specific mental notes of details that they share with you about upcoming surgeries, job interviews, praise reports, etc. And, imagine if you even prayed for them right there on the spot? Remember, no one is expecting you to personally care for every single person. But, if you make it a point to use your time intentionally, there will be great reward. Not to mention the fact that when you

WHAT IF YOU TOOK EVEN JUST ONE HOUR EACH WEEK TO GO HAVE COFFEE WITH SOMEONE IN YOUR CONGREGATION WHO HAS NOTHING TO OFFER YOU OR YOUR MINISTRY?

are on stage looking out, it allows you to have an even more personal connection with these special people. We encourage you to set some goals for every Sunday concerning pastoral care. It's also a good idea to encourage your worship team members to participate in these goals as well.

What if you took even just one hour each week to go have coffee with someone in your congregation who has nothing to offer you or your ministry? Actually, taking a moment just to hear their story may completely impact your life and inspire you as a leader in a new way. Find an elderly couple and invite them out to dinner with your spouse and just sit and listen to their life and marriage story. I promise you that the time spent with them will not return void. This also allows your spouse to be a part of your pastoral ministry behind the scenes and will help them understand why you love what you do so much.

All of this falls under the responsibility of the pastoral care that all who bear the name of Jesus are called to fulfill. We need to stop making this about a line item on our job descriptions and realize that this is desired by God to be a way of life. Okay, now put this book down for a moment and reach out to the person or people in your congregation that have already come to your mind and get something on the calendar! This makes all the difference.

CONCLUSION

One of the most important things that you can experience on

your journey as a worship pastor is your transition from a music leader to a shepherd. This really isn't optional. There are many ways you can pastor well from the stage, but the relationships you build in your community over time will see some of the greatest fruit. Our churches are desperate for more pastors, not rockstars. We will only be able to pastor well if we are willing to surrender our aspirations to "be something special" and choose to devote our energy to loving the people around us.

Don't let anyone look down on you because you are young, but set an example for the believers in speech, in conduct, in love, in faith and in purity.

1 TIMOTHY 4:12

CHAPTER 10

The Heart of the Worship Pastor

YOU ARE NOT ALONE

We understand that on any given Sunday it is very possible that your smile and passion for worship from the stage is not always a reflection of what is "truly" going on in your heart and your life. Do you ever feel like a counterfeit? Do you ever feel like a fraud or even a professional worship actor? Do you ever feel underqualified or even that your personal life disqualifies you from stepping one foot up on that stage? Well, if you have felt any of these to be true about yourself, you are not alone.

Have you ever felt ashamed to be leading God's people because of some secret sin in your life? Maybe you have felt like a hypocrite because of what you have been looking at on your phone, or maybe you had too much to drink the night before at a party. What about your marriage? Have you ever led worship on the morning after a fight you had with your spouse the night before that was still unresolved? Well, if any of this is true, you are not alone!

What about an unresolved and unreconciled conflict with a family member or friend? Have you ever felt guilty about singing songs about God's grace and forgiveness towards you yet being unwilling to extend that same grace and forgiveness to another? If any of this resonates with you, you are not alone! Most of your fellow worship pastors can truly relate.

From the beginning of this book you have listened to Josh and me rattling on and on about many things concerning worship and ministry that we are both very passionate about. But you must know and understand that none of this matters compared to what you are about to read in this final chapter. Everything about what you do and how you serve your King comes down to what we call the CORE (your true character). You must also know that it would be sin for us NOT to share this and to make this the highest priority for this book (James 4:17). The heart of the worship pastor is the top priority of Likewise Worship and is in essence where I came up with the name and brand. As the Church in the New Testament was growing and developing, the apostle Paul and Jesus' disciples would live out the Gospel and set a standard to encourage their followers and readers of their letters to "go and do likewise." This way of living was introduced to me when my grandfather decided to be more than just a grandpa to me.

He set out to make me a disciple of Jesus and it wasn't just what he said that helped change the course of my life, it was how he lived. Because of his influence in my life and his example of a transformed and sold out life for Christ, I have made it my mission to "go and do likewise."

Our hope and prayer is that the knowledge you gain from this book will become wisdom as you put what you know into action. It is easy to sound smart and even look smart in our "knowledge saturated" world, but it's another thing when your life actually bears healthy fruit when you live out the truths that are only found in the Word of God!

I want to live in such a way
That the day will come when my children say
"He was not always perfect, but it's true of our dad:
He lived up to the knowledge he had."
Live up to the knowledge you have,
In obedience to what God has said.
Let His will be done in all that you do.
In thought and in word and in all your deeds too.
Keep growing in grace, and the wisdom of faith,
And live up to the knowledge you have.
- - Larry Wright (my grandpa)

ON THE FRONT LINES

When many people surrender their lives to Christ and commit to following Him, they don't truly realize what they are actually following Him into. But typically, after a few months on our spiritual journey, most of us find ourselves in the midst of a raging battle. Ephesians 6 is clear that this war that we are fighting is not against a brutal and scary human dictator that sends his armies into your city to slaughter thousands of men, women, and children. Oh no, it is actually worse than that. This is a battle against the extremely powerful supernatural forces in a different realm that are all around us. Someone once told me that if I could put on a pair of "spiritual realm" glasses to really see what is going on around me, I would be so frightened to the point of throwing those glasses far from my face and then running to the restroom to change my soiled pants! Okay, that may be a bit extreme and too specific. However, we MUST face the reality that this battle is real and has been going on for thousands of years. One of the reasons why I love the Lord of the Rings movies so much is because of the battle scenes. Those incomprehensible and intense scenes depict where my imagination goes when I think of the spiritual battle we are in. Yikes!

To be honest with you, I was completely ignorant and unaware of the spiritual warfare going on around me until I first stepped into music ministry when I was 18. It was like a switch turned on, and it seemed as though every time I turned a corner on my journey with Christ, I was faced with a violent attack from the enemy! These attacks manifested themselves in so many different ways. Sometimes it was random dark thoughts that would secretly enter my mind at unexpected times concerning my soul, my faith, and my identity. Sometimes it was an oppressive spirit that would leave me feeling physically and mentally paralyzed and deeply fearful throughout the night. And even at times these attacks would come through the hurtful words and actions of people in my community that would often cause me to struggle with depression and doubt. I seriously feel that even since Josh and I began writing this book, we both have experienced attacks in various ways from the enemy to try to steer us off course and distract us.

I say all this to remind you that, in general, we as believers are all at war with an enemy that hates us and hates the fact that we have committed our lives and gifts to serving in God's Kingdom. He will do anything to destroy our witness and to diminish the value of our calling.

Where this gets even more challenging to talk about is the fact that we are not only in a battle as image-bearers of God, but we are standing on THE FRONT LINES of this battle as pastors and ministry leaders. Behind us stands a multitude of God's people that we are called to lead and it is important that we hold that front line firmly.

Our job on the front lines is to unite the King's army as we lead them in a unified battle cry and song declaring the power, the glory, and the victory that has already been set before us by our King. Even though we seem to be outnumbered and, at times, completely surrounded by the vast army that stands against us, we can rest in the beautiful truth and faithful promise that our King goes before us as our commander and protector. His Word alone is enough to conquer the enemy before us.

One of the main reasons we love giving pastors these images to ponder is because it is so important for each of us to know that we do not stand alone on the front lines. When you look to your left and to your right, you will see faithful servants of the King armed and ready to hold the line with you. YOU ARE NOT ALONE!

Knowing that you are on the front lines can be so scary at times even if you understand that there are so many others with you, especially since the ones on the front lines are usually the first ones to get an arrow through the chest. Or a spear through the head...or a...okay, maybe I have seen too many battle movies. Seriously though, this is why we have to allow the Word of God to be our hope, peace, and assurance in the battle. So let's remind ourselves of what we need to do as pastors to make sure we are fully equipped for the battle.

ARMOR OF GOD - EPHESIANS 6:10-17
10 Finally, be strong in the Lord and in His mighty power. 11 Put on the full armor of God, so that you can take your stand against the devil's schemes. 12 For our struggle is not against flesh and blood, but against the rulers, against the authorities, against

the powers of this dark world and against the spiritual forces of evil in the heavenly realms. 13 Therefore put on the full armor of God, so that when the day of evil comes, you may be able to stand your ground, and after you have done everything, to stand. 14 Stand firm then, with the belt of truth buckled around your waist, with the breastplate of righteousness in place, 15 and with your feet fitted with the readiness that comes from the gospel of peace. 16 In addition to all this, take up the shield of faith, with which you can extinguish all the flaming arrows of the evil one. 17 Take the helmet of salvation and the sword of the Spirit, which is the word of God.

RESISTING THE ENEMY - 1 Peter 5:8-9
8 Be alert and of sober mind. Your enemy the devil prowls around like a roaring lion looking for someone to devour. 9 Resist him, standing firm in the faith, because you know that the family of believers throughout the world is undergoing the same kind of sufferings.

OUR BEST WEAPON

In order to resist and defend against an enemy, it is important to have an understanding of their schemes and tactics. From what we can see throughout the whole story of Scripture, we know that the devil is a liar. And this enemy of ours often deploys different tactics with the goal of getting us to do two things: doubt God and depend on ourselves.

In the Garden, the serpent accomplished this by getting Eve to believe that God didn't have her best interest in mind. It seemed for a moment as if God was holding out on what was really "good." In that moment, Eve doubted God's goodness and reached for the fruit from the Tree of the Knowledge of Good and Evil to have this "understanding" for herself. And, the consequences of Eve's rebellion have been felt throughout history.

The tactics and goals of our enemy are no different today. The lies just take different shapes. In order to combat the lies of the enemy, there is only one weapon fit for the job: truth. Specifically, the truth found in God's Word.

Jesus took one weapon into battle with the enemy in Matthew 4. To Jesus, the best defenses against the schemes of His enemy were the commandments of His Father.

Jesus was tempted to doubt God and depend on Himself for His hunger, His reputation, and His glory.

In a similar way, our enemy wants to lure us into a lifetime of distrusting God and making our own way through the world.

One of the greatest ways I see this happening among believers has a lot to do with our current culture. I see this lie entering the hearts of many people dressed like this:

How can we really know what the authors of Scripture really meant?

Who are we to say that we know how to interpret God's Word?

You are arrogant if you claim to know what God's Word means and that it is the only source of truth.

This clearly isn't how the Apostle Paul treated what He knew then as the Scriptures (2 Timothy 3:16) or the teachings of Jesus. They were a lifeline, the basis for morality and training in right living. When we believe that we can't trust God's Word, we are left to the wind. We are dead leaves off of an autumn tree. We spend our lives in spiritual limbo, never knowing what the "right" thing is. We bring a paper sword to the fight of our lives.

We *firmly* believe that God's Word is a reliable guide and compass for life. We understand that there are many interpretations of different passages and many questions that we all still have. We see through a mirror dimly, as Paul did. Our point is that the Word of God is worth studying, believing, and trusting. The more we know it, trust it, and obey it, the greater bearings we will have in our own lives. We want to become the types of people for whom doing the right thing is the natural thing to do.

The Word of God is our weapon against the lies of the enemy. May we know it and use it.

TRAINING FOR RIGHTEOUSNESS

Seeing the Word of God as a double-edged sword (Hebrews 4:12) gives us such a great illustration to think about as we are using it in the battle for our minds and hearts. I often think about how frustrating it would be if, in the heat of battle, I found my weapon to be dull or that I was not equipped to use it effectively. We need to make sure we understand that a good soldier works hard to be fully equipped, trained, and conditioned before the battle.

So much of this comes down to our spiritual and mental health! Are we spending enough time training in godliness and righteousness (1 Tim 4:7,8)? Do we "work out" the spiritual muscles that are essential in holding up our armor and carrying our shield and sword? Just as we are commanded by God to be physically healthy and to take care of our earthly bodies where the Spirit of the Lord dwells, we must take seriously the calling to be spiritually healthy, conditioned, and equipped.

For the purpose of being prepared and ready for the battle, the first place we can turn when it comes to equipping ourselves is Psalm 1. If there is anyone that can relate to us as worship pastors and soldiers for Christ, it is King David. This man truly personified and connected with so much of what today's worship pastors face in church ministry! Here are a few of the parallels between worship pastors and the ministry of

King David: He was first chosen and called by God to step into a role that he could only accomplish with God by his side. He was gifted with a supernatural musical ability that could calm the hearts of those who listen and, at the same time, cause demons to flee! He was granted the ability to write lyrics and poems that would supernaturally speak to and inspire a thousand generations. He suffered great loss, tragedy, and sorrow, yet kept a steadfast heart. And finally, after falling deep into temptation and committing the most unthinkable offenses, he was able to overcome the intense amount of guilt, shame, and depression that one can imagine by grasping and trusting the fullness of God's grace.

This is why the words of David in Psalm 1 can be so beautifully instrumental and trusted on our leadership journey.

How blessed is the man who does not walk in the counsel of the wicked, nor stand in the path of sinners, nor sit in the seat of scoffers! But his delight is in the law of the Lord, and in His law he meditates day and night. He will be like a tree firmly planted by streams of water, which yields its fruit in its season. And its leaf does not wither; and in whatever he does, he prospers. Psalm 1

WALK - STAND - SIT

One thing that has always struck me about that passage was the progression of the man into sin. You read that he walks with sin, then he's standing in sin, and then he finishes by sitting comfortably in it.

But this pattern was all determined by one thing: his source of counsel, his source of wisdom! David is contrasting two different people in this Psalm. The first listened to the counsel of the wicked and walked in it. This person eventually found themselves comfortably set in their sinful ways.

Pay attention to the other man that David describes. This man had no special skills. This man has no special privileges. The only thing we know about this other man was that he spent day and night meditating on the law of God. And what was the result? This man is firmly planted, yielding fruit, and prospering in whatever he does.

The Word of God forms us like nothing else can. The Law is God's gift to you and I. It is a blueprint for human flourishing in the middle of a broken and sinful world. When we meditate on it day and night, we become the types of people who know what to do and how to honor God.

YOU WILL BE LIKE A TREE

Sometimes in the winter season, I can paddle out in the Pacific on my surfboard and look east to see the beautiful snow-covered San Gabriel Mountains. It is truly an inspiring moment when I am looking up to those peaceful mountains and at

the same time experiencing the vastness of the ocean and the power of the crashing waves all around me. I also think about how cool it is that the snow will soon melt and make its way all the way down to where I am surfing sometime in the Spring. When I let my imagination run wild with the process and journey that the melted snow takes, I am brought back into the picture that David is painting in this first Psalm. I think about that tree that sits firmly planted beside the streams of water. If I were a tree and could choose where I could live, the obvious choice would be right there near that mountain stream. The constant nutrients that are carried down the mountain through the water currents for me to feed on and soak in to my roots would surely make for a healthy and fruitful life!

I can just imagine David himself, sitting on a rock, listening to this peaceful stream and looking at the beautiful trees around him as he writes these compelling comparisons of life. All of this wisdom can lead us into a truly prosperous and abundant life! When Jesus said in John 10:10 "I come that they may have life and have it abundantly," I truly believe that this abundant life can be attained by putting into practice those simple words from David's heart, by meditating on God's Word and obeying it. If we allow the Word of the Lord to be our foundation by meditating on it day and night, we will have what it takes to overcome the wickedness in the world just as Josh explained earlier about Jesus in the wilderness. This is the strengthening and equipping that we are talking about when it comes to this battle we are in.

PRODUCING FRUIT

This big and healthy tree, whose roots grow strong and deep and are fed by a reliable source of nutrition, will bear much fruit. It is God's desire for us that as a result of this process, we too will bear good fruit. So, as we approach the end of this book, it is extremely important to examine the fruit we are bearing in our lives and ministry. At the beginning of this chapter we addressed some questions that are obviously the result of bad fruit in the life of the worship pastor. This bad fruit is what leads many of us into burnout, depression, and eventually abandoning our post in church ministry.

We need to understand that bad fruit in our lives is always preceded by a lack of nutrients or some sort of impurity that has worked its way into our root system. It is important to identify this bad fruit and to cut it off of the tree. Sometimes we have to even cut off an entire branch that has been infected so that healing can begin. This is called pruning. Without going into detail and identifying the potential bad fruit in our lives, you must remember that you are not alone and that every tree will bear bad fruit at one time or another. The best way to prune your life of this bad fruit is to ask for help, and to allow someone to walk alongside you.

We also have to understand that good fruit and bad fruit don't happen in a vacuum! They're a result of a certain kind of life. Good fruit is a result of a tree whose roots have properly absorbed nutrients from a healthy water source. Here are some practical ways to keep your tree healthy and bearing good fruit:

- **Reading and Meditating on God's Word:** don't let this be cliche. It is our lifeline. We encourage you to make this a practice throughout your entire day.

- **Prayer:** Bring your whole life to God who sustains you and cares for you. Process your whole life before the one who formed you and knows you intimately. Stop to listen. Make regular, scheduled time for this.

- **Mentorship:** Go find someone to disciple and mentor you!

- **Sleep:** Don't underestimate how much a lack of physical rest can impact your spiritual and emotional life.

- **Sabbath:** Schedule and commit to one 24-hour period each week to stop your work, enjoy God, and do the things that refresh you. God commands it.

- **Forgiveness:** A lack of forgiveness will eat you away. Keep short accounts and extend what has been endlessly extended to you.

- **Confession:** Confession brings healing (1 John 1:9). As soon as sin creeps into your life, confess it to God. Don't let it linger. As soon as you realize that you have sinned against someone else, go confess to them and seek reconciliation.

- **Community:** We live in a very individualized culture. But we weren't meant to follow Jesus by ourselves. We need people in our lives who can see our blind spots, hold us accountable, encourage us, and help us persevere to the end.

Jesus said that we prove to be His disciples when we "bear fruit" (John 15:8). Knowing Jesus and becoming like Him has to be our greatest priority.

In addition to these spiritual disciplines and practices, we would like to provide some other practical thoughts and insights pertaining to our lives as disciples of Jesus.

A FOOLISH SACRIFICE

We need to address the fact that most pastors struggle with balance in their ministry, specifically in the area of marriage and parenting. I recently heard a pastor share his struggle as a father and husband while trying to lead his massive church. He repented of the fact that, for so many years, he knowingly put his own family on the altar of the local church and watched them burn. He woke up one day feeling deeply convicted that those who were gifted to him by God Himself to hold the highest priority in this life had been sacrificed for an ego-driven career in ministry that left him feeling empty. The storms of reality came without warning and he watched his home crumble along with the sandcastle church kingdom he was building. It was so sad.

No pastor ever sets out to destroy their own families for the furthering of their ministry career or their pastoral duty. It just happens. It actually happens all the time. It's what some call "the slow fade." What most pastors don't realize is that there is actually a simple and common sense way to prevent this from happening to them. The best way to explain this is by giving you these three things to remember:

1. REMEMBER, you are actually not that important. I don't even feel bad about saying that. We all struggle in ministry with the sin of people-pleasing and thinking that so much about the spiritual wellbeing of others in our church depends on us as the pastors. WRONG! The spiritual wellbeing of the ones that the Lord has placed in your home are to be your highest priority. Once our homes are healthy and secure, we can be a blessing to others in our community. We need to take a serious look at our motives as we serve in the Church and make sure that our priorities are in balance.

Helpful tip - It's actually beneficial for some of you to write out the actual amount of hours, days, weeks, and months that you are spending with your spouse and with your children compared to the church community. This is helpful to look at and to share with the mentors in your life for accountability and wisdom.

2. REMEMBER, God's Kingdom (The Church) will continue on just fine without you. If we are honest with ourselves, we all

struggle with the desire of feeling needed in some way. It just feels good to know we have something to offer that people need. However, we must work hard to fight against this attack on our identities. The enemy loves to tempt and entice pastors to believe that "we are what we do" as Josh will explain at the end of this chapter. We must always remember that what the people in our church communities "need" most is Jesus. The sooner you can point them to Him, the less pressure you will feel to make sure everyone is happy.

Helpful Tip - Think about where your value lies. Stop letting your desire to meet the needs of the people in your church community keep you from fulfilling God's greater purpose for His Kingdom.

3. REMEMBER, the health of your marriage and your family is actually a true reflection of your own spiritual health, your overall character, and your character as a leader. Have you ever stopped to think about the fact that the Gospel can best be grasped and understood by those around you simply by observing your relationship with your spouse? The marriage between a man and a woman is such a perfect example of God's love and redemption. How can a man preach the forgiveness of sins and reconciliation with God and yet turn around and not extend that same grace and forgiveness to his wife? What an awesome opportunity to put the Gospel on display within our marriages!

What about your children? Are they spoiled and out of control? Are their hearts disciplined and their lives on the path of righteousness? We could go on and on for pages talking about the amazing opportunity to put God's love and grace on display through our families.

You are hopefully beginning to see why the rest of this chapter is so important. If the enemy can take down your marriage and your children, your witness for the Gospel will be diminished and your credibility to speak for it will be compromised.

PREVENTATIVE MEASURES

One practical way that my wife, Falon, and I are daily bulletproofing our marriage is by over communicating, especially in church ministry and even when it's difficult to talk about. I can't even count the number of times where there have been awkward and uncomfortable interactions between myself and another woman either in the church community or on staff. This is why ever since the beginning, I made a commitment to tell Falon everything. Yes, everything. We both learned early on in our relationship that the devil hates it when we communicate with each other, especially the things that could lead to destruction. Here is a little quote from my wife on this matter:

I have always been very thankful that Justin and I have open communication in our marriage, especially regarding women in the church that don't have boundaries and are needy. I know women naturally look up to men that are in a spiritual leadership role. Justin has always been honest with me about every situation he has encountered that the enemy could use to cause division. It has also made me aware of how I can be praying for my husband who is on the front lines and constantly under attack. This has protected and safeguarded us and our marriage in more ways than I can count. - - Falon Unger

RED FLAG ALERT! - While we are on this topic regarding the ministry interaction with the opposite sex, here are a couple of things to consider:

- Did you know that singing a duet, harmonizing, or even simply sharing the lead role on stage with someone of the opposite sex can be compared to an intimate slow dance together with that person? Yikes! The eye contact, smiling interactions, the movement of the notes, and the spiritual connection that takes place when a man and woman sing together can become personal and dangerous. Put all this together with someone who is tired, has a strained or stagnant marriage, or is at a point of distress and depression, and it could be a recipe for disaster. We must be cautious and see these interactions as a way for the enemy to plant little seeds that will surely grow into something awful. Maybe you can relate and these seeds have already taken root in your life in some way. Stop reading right now and communicate

this with your spouse or someone that you trust to hold you accountable.

- If you are married, don't be alone with the opposite sex. *Ever.* It is worth it to be above reproach in this area. We have seen even the most innocent interactions between a man and a woman in church ministry turn into a devastating blow up for the individuals and the church community. It can be such a frustrating mess.

- Let's get even more personal for a moment. Your smartphone can be one of your greatest tools for your ministry, but also more destructive than a hand grenade! It is always better not to have conversations with the opposite sex through text unless you have a witness or a third party attached to the message. It is also very difficult to clean up the huge problems that we create with our smartphones.

These types of temptations don't only exist for married worship pastors. Whether you are single or married, you are looked at in a certain light when you take the stage. Be aware, once again, that there is a target on your back.

If you are a single worship pastor, know that the way you interact with the opposite sex is under the microscope. Chances are, you will get a lot of attention because you are on stage. How you handle that attention is so important.

Our encouragement to you is to always be intentional. Do your best to never put yourself in a situation (whether in-person, text, or any other form of communication) where an action of yours could be misinterpreted. This is one of the greatest ways that the enemy can distract us from our roles in ministry.

When it comes to sin in your life in this area (and every area), don't believe the lie that since "everyone struggles with this" you can let it have a place in your life. Jesus taught it most clearly: cutting out the sin in your life is worth whatever it takes (Matt. 5:27-30).

REST UP

We are called to be above reproach or in other words, without blame, as leaders in the church. So, we must do the hard work of protecting our hearts and minds on a daily basis. Many ministry leaders make foolish and impure decisions because they have allowed themselves to become exhausted in their work. Stop it! God gave us this gift and commandment called "sabbath." Sabbath rest is a powerful weapon we can use to combat our busy world. God Himself established this rhythm of work and rest. And when we follow His intended rhythm, we find that we can actually be more productive in His Kingdom if we just stop and rest.

Do you know how to effectively rest and go on vacation with your family? I do. But I had to learn the hard way. In my early

years as a worship pastor, even though I was given three weeks of paid vacation per year, I deeply struggled with "turning off." I actually mean that in two ways--turning off my mind and turning off my phone. This was a big problem for me already, but what made it so difficult for me as a pastor was that my boss required me to keep my phone with me in case something goes wrong with the guest worship leader or the church services while I was away. This made for a very rough first couple of years in ministry for me as I tried to figure out my place on staff, how to honor authority, and how to put my family first. Unfortunately, these pressures from the senior pastor and the church caused me to develop some bad habits that took me a while to overcome. Eventually, I had to man up and let my boss know that I love my wife and my kids more than I love him and the church community. Bottom line: if your church leadership doesn't allow you to completely disconnect when you are on vacation or even observing your weekly sabbath day, it might be time to put your foot down and have some tough conversations. It is important for all leaders in the church to have a strong sense of self awareness and an ever growing sense of their true identity.

A FINAL WORD ON IDENTITY

As we bring this book to a close, we must be aware of one of the most important battlegrounds in our lives: our sense of identity. What we believe about who we are determines what we do in life. When we trust the Word of God and His promises to be our source of identity, we experience freedom. But, when we begin to believe that we are what we can accomplish, worship ministry becomes challenging.

We firmly believe that you cannot pastor well until you understand the true source of your identity.

In order to truly claim and live out our identity as children of God made in the image of God, we MUST detach ourselves from our existing sources of identity. For me personally, I was attached to my identity as a worship leader.

Deep down, I believed that I was only as valuable as how well I "performed" as a worship leader. If I'm not a good worship leader, then who am I?

I didn't realize this was the case until I graduated from college and evaluated the ministry I had done up until that point. Much of my ministry was characterized by pressure, fear, frustration, and even regret. In the midst of all of that, God did amazing things and I truly had a heart to worship Him alone.

But as I began to process my experience in ministry, a lot of it felt more like a stressful job than a blessing. What began as something I really loved had become a source of anxiety. Something was wrong.

After wrestling with this for a while, I realized that God won't share His glory. And this was my core problem. Me getting glory and God getting glory at the same time doesn't work.

What I didn't realize was that part of me was building my own kingdom. While this was unintentional, and I love Jesus and what He has done for me, it was slowly having a negative impact on all that I did.

It manifested itself in these ways:

- Being really concerned with what people thought of me.
- Critiquing every moment of every worship set to the smallest detail.
- Being hard on my team for the sake of "excellence"... aka my reputation…
- Getting frustrated when we did not completely nail the set feeling anxiety about every worship set because I wanted to be seen as a good leader.

When I came to terms with some of these things, I was broken. I even had to call a few of the people I served with in the past to ask forgiveness for the ways I treated them as their leader!

If you have ever felt any of these things before, you are not alone! Here's the most incredible part: God wants to free you from that. He has done that for me.

And the freedom God gives is found in living for His kingdom. When we realize that we are not the sum of what we can do or accomplish, we are free to give ourselves wholly to God's mission and trust Him with all of the work to be done.

You are not what you do! You are a child of God, made in the image of God, useful in the kingdom of God. And when God's glory becomes our highest priority, then we are truly free people.

You must remember that the enemy is after your heart, your sense of identity. Your awareness of the presence of this enemy and his army is crucial for your service in the King's army. May we always commit ourselves to building God's kingdom, not our own.

I recently heard this statement: "It is entirely possible in our culture to have a successful ministry while having zero spiritual depth."

This should make us all pause.

Am I really following Jesus?

Do I lead worship because of my heart for my Lord and His body? Or is it my personal platform?

Am I building my life on the rock of obedience to Jesus' teachings or the sand of superficial spirituality?

The answers to these questions will influence the impact and longevity of your ministry. Jesus invites us all to live for His kingdom and not our own. When we seek first His kingdom, we'll find that we have all we need.

FINAL ENCOURAGEMENTS

In the movie *STAR WARS: The Rise Of Skywalker*, there is a scene that has profoundly impacted the way we look at Likewise Worship as a ministry. Members of the Resistance had their backs against the wall, wondering if any help would come. When all seemed hopeless, one character encouraged the Resistance with this statement: "The enemy wins by making you think that you are alone." WOW, does this relate to us as ministry leaders or what? It's so important that you understand who goes before you and who is walking with you as you navigate through this ever-changing world in ministry to the saints.

We want you to know that we are with you! You are not on an island left to survive on your own. One of the main reasons that Likewise Worship exists is to be a space for worship leaders and worship pastors to remember that fact. We encourage you to take advantage of any community you are a part of and to remember that our doors are always open.

As the world continues to grow darker and more divided with every passing day, we urge you to daily consider your calling as a soldier of Christ and your position on the front lines. Use your heart for worship and passion for music to unite those

around you in your community and the local church around the Gospel. Whether you are gathering together in a home with 20 people or a worship center with 2000, the Gospel lived out through the local church is still a beacon of hope for the world. And it is an honor that we get to be a part of this together.

If anyone, then, knows the good they ought to do and doesn't do it, it is sin for them. JAMES 4:17

MORE HELPFUL RESOURCES FOR WORSHIP PASTORS

The Ruthless Elimination of Hurry - **John Mark Comer**

A Long Obedience in the Same Direction - **Eugene Peterson**

New Morning Mercies - **Paul David Tripp**

Rhythms of Grace - **Mike Cosper**

Our Own Hymn Book - **Charles Spurgeon**

In the Name of Jesus - **Henri Nouwen**

Spirit of the Disciplines - **Dallas Willard**

The Discipline of Grace - **Jerry Bridges**

The Meaning of Marriage - **Tim Keller**

Disappearing Church - **Mark Sayers**

You Are What You Love - **James K.A. Smith**

Emotionally Healthy Spirituality - **Pete Scazzero**

The Knowledge of the Holy - **A.W. Tozer**

ABOUT THE AUTHORS

Justin has been committed to the local church for over 15 years as a worship pastor. Passionate about unifying the Body of Christ with the gift of music, he has learned to stand firm amidst the cultural and traditional challenges that many churches face in regards to worship and the Sunday gathering. He is a pastor of pastors and has a heart to disciple, equip, and encourage both young and seasoned worship leaders that are called to serve the local church.

Justin serves primarily as the Executive Director with Likewise Worship and also as a Worship Leader, Speaker and Consultant for churches that are struggling to bring all generations together in worship.

He currently resides in Huntington Beach with his wife Falon, and their 4 beautiful children.

JUSTIN UNGER

Josh has been leading worship and growing as a pastor for over a decade. A graduate of Grand Canyon University with a BA in Christian Studies, he has a heart for discipleship, particularly for investing in young worship leaders. Josh serves as a part-time worship pastor for Hope Church in Phoenix, Arizona.

Josh serves primarily as the Lead Director with Likewise Worship, helping oversee the Phoenix collective gatherings, the ministry vision and curriculum, and all of our Likewise area directors.

Josh and his wife Brynne currently live in Phoenix, AZ.

JOSH JAMES

ACKNOWLEDGEMENTS

JUSTIN
WOULD LIKE TO THANK. . .

My amazing wife, Falon, who continues to faithfully put on display God's love, patience and kindness! I am honored to have you by my side on this adventure of serving our King. Thank you for being steadfast in the Lord and for your patience with me as I have poured countless hours into this book and ministry! You will never know how deep my love is for you and how much you inspire me to be more like Christ every day!

My three crazy awesome sons, Carson, Nolan & Eli. I am honored to be your father and am so proud of the men you are becoming in Christ.

My beautiful princess, Ethnie, who resembles the kindness and peace of Jesus in so many ways! I can clearly see the Spirit of God alive in each of your lives every day!

Josh, for taking a risk and walking with me on this Likewise Worship adventure. Your love and commitment to the Word of God is so inspiring. Thank you for your teachable and humble heart and for your patience with the crazy dude behind the wheel! We love you and Brynne more than you can know and are so thankful for your friendship.

JOSH
WOULD LIKE TO THANK. . .

My sweet wife, Brynne, who has been an incredible supporter and encourager of not only me but this ministry. Thank you for all of your patience during the late nights of writing and editing and all of the work trips, and for all of the ways you inspire me to be like Jesus! It is so fun to be on this journey with you!

My parents, Jim and Ruth, who have supported and encouraged this project and process in more ways than I can count. Thank you for "teaching me in the way I should go" and for being faithful friends and mentors every step of the way.

Justin, for believing in me as a teenager and pouring endless wisdom into my life. Your influence on my life is far-reaching and I am a better man and disciple of Jesus because of being on this journey with you! Thank you for the opportunity to join you on this mission. And Falon Unger, for being a great friend, mentor, and example of a pastor's wife to Brynne. We love you both!

JUSTIN & JOSH
WOULD ALSO LIKE TO THANK. . .

All of our Active Likewise Members, who inspire and encourage us to keep going on this mission. Your availability, vulnerability, and participation on this journey with us has helped us better understand our roles as pastors and followers of Jesus! Thank you for your support and for all that you do for the local church.

The faithful Likewise supporters, donors, church partners and prayer team. So much of the impact that this ministry is having is because of your generosity and support. We are forever grateful to have you on mission with us.

And finally, all of those who took the time to read the first few drafts of this book and for your invaluable feedback and encouragement.

LIKEWISE WORSHIP

DEVELOPING HEALTHY AND HUMBLE WORSHIP PASTORS

PROMOTING A BIBLICAL HEART OF WORSHIP IN THE LOCAL CHURCH

OUR MISSION

We believe that worship culture and philosophy is set and maintained by the worship pastor. Likewise exists for the development, discipleship, and mentoring of this next generation of worship pastors and their families. The goal of our time spent with these leaders is to raise up those who can lead a multi-generational gathering with a shepherd's heart. We pour into these worship leaders in three distinct ways: monthly gatherings, one-on-one discipleship, and annual retreats.

If you are a worship pastor interested in joining the Likewise Worship community, please visit: www.likewiseworship.com and click the JOIN button.

Or send an email to info@likewiseworship.com

Likewise Worship Inc. is a 501 C3 Non-profit Ministry
Tax ID # 83-2544594

Your tax deductible donations will go to serve churches all
across the United States through the worship pastors that we are
discipling and sending.

Please prayerfully consider how you might be led by the Lord to
support the Likewise Worship Mission.

To give by Credit Card: Visit www.likewiseworship.com/donate
To give by Check: Make payable to Likewise Worship Inc.
Mail to: Likewise Worship
                                     419 Main St., suite 150
                                     Huntington Beach, CA 92648
For donation questions contact us at: nina@likewiseworship.com

FOOTNOTES

1 https://www.etymonline.com/word/pastor

2 https://usatoday30.usatoday.com/news/offbeat/2005-07-08-sheep-suicide_x.htm

3 Eugene Peterson, A Long Obedience in the Same Direction (Downers Grove, IL: InterVarsity Press, 2000), 13

4 https://www.desiringgod.org/messages/present-your-bodies-as-a-living-sacrifice-to-goD

5 Eugene Peterson, A Long Obedience in the Same Direction (Downers Grove, IL: InterVarsity Press, 2000), 54

6 https://www.sleepfoundation.org/bedroom-environment/hear/what-white-noise

7 Charles Spurgeon, Our Own Hymnbook (London, England: Passmore and Alabaster, 1883), vi.